WE CAN because WE THINK WE CAN

TERI KUZMA

Balboa Press books may be ordered through booksellers or by contacting:

Balboa Press
A Division of Hay House
1663 Liberty Drive
Bloomington, IN 47403
www.balboapress.com
1 (877) 407-4847

Because of the dynamic nature of the Internet, any web addresses or links contained in this book may have changed since publication and may no longer be valid. The views expressed in this work are solely those of the author and do not necessarily reflect the views of the publisher, and the publisher hereby disclaims any responsibility for them.

Any people depicted in stock imagery provided by Thinkstock are models, and such images are being used for illustrative purposes only.
Certain stock imagery © Thinkstock.

ISBN: 978-1-5043-3305-4 (sc)
ISBN: 978-1-5043-3304-7 (e)

Print information available on the last page.

Balboa Press rev. date: 06/08/2015

BALBOA
PRESS
A DIVISION OF HAY HOUSE

This Book is Dedicated to:

My father, Andrew Paul Kuzma 2/04/1910 2/20/1975 God gave me the ability,
my father gave me confidence and taught me how to use my ability.

and

My two sons who have been there for me.

On the cover of the book is a butterfly and cocoon.

*Many years ago I read an article on a moth trying to emerge from its cocoon. A man thought
he would help and made a cut in the cocoon, which allowed the moth to emerge easily, without
a **struggle.**   As a result the moths wings never developed and it spent its life dragging
around a shriveled wings and a swollen body. **Struggle** might be what we need to succeed.*

Table of Contents

Chapter One

If YOU WANT TO ...... YOU CAN

- Do you have dreams of a different life? I did!

- Do you dream you had a marriage to a kind, considerate husband? *However*, you are stuck in a miserable, unhappy, abusive marriage and can see no way out. You have children, responsibilities, bills, etc.

- Do you think as a single woman, you can't do many things without a man?

- Do you feel trapped in a job you can hardly muster the energy to get up and go to every day ? Perhaps you are having problems with your boss, you feel unappreciated and would like to quit but you need the money.

- Do you read very slow, misspell words, reverse numbers and letters?

- You would like to be an artist but that's a luxury.

- Do you dream of travel to foreign countries to learn about their culture?

- The answer? Win the lottery *then* things would be different *but* ...

You get the idea ... there just isn't any way you can even afford to dream, let alone think about how you can make your dreams come true. *I know where you are, I was there, I was all the above.* So what can you do? Where or how do you start?

First, I know I *must* make changes in my life. I'm nobody special, don't have connections with anyone, have very little money and have no idea where or how to begin but I will! *I don't want to turn 60 or 70 years old and say "I wish I had ..... "* It is up to me, *God* has given me a brain, I thank my father for teaching me how to use it. Now it was up to me to figure out how to make these dreams come true.

Being open to possibilities, you can change your life. Anything is possible, it's not going to be easy and support won't always be there for you. For me, there were struggles, a few failures and unexpected things that happened, some great, some a little frightening, all unforgettable experiences. Perhaps, this book will give you ideas on how you too can change your life. Maybe it will give you the courage, inspiration, strength, some skills and ideas on how you can make **your** dreams come true. It will also teach you how to make positive changes by helping you change your thinking in how you approach challenges in your life. Please remember, anything is possible - but you have to *want change, ask God for help*, then figure out how you are going to make it happen.

This is a diary account of my life. I have had an adventurous, wonderful, exciting life and would like to share the second half of my life story with you. By using the ability ***God gave all of us*** to work hard and think creatively, we can change our lives to the life we want. I've included color pictures of interesting, different people, places and happenings. Although they look different, in every location the people were friendly. Most of all, I hope it will help you to enjoy the life you want to live. WE CAN because WE THINK WE CAN. This is my adventure with life.

"The first step toward success is taken when you refuse to be a captive of the environment in which you first find yourself." - Mark Caine

Chapter Two

Time For Change

After three years of trying again in a new location, survival meant it was time for a divorce. He was very charming publicly, friends and family didn't know the problems or the fear we lived in. My sons and I never talked with people about our life at home.

* * * *

Now working at the office of a private psychologist who wanted someone on his staff to work with the learning disabled. I worked with some of his clients plus recruited new students. We were supposed to work as a team and once there were enough students, I was to hire a new teacher. The business was growing. Began to ask myself, why couldn't I start my own business? *Yes, why not?*

I had studied, read, attended seminars and researched all the current information on the learning disabled for years. Had worked in a school system and was now working for this Psychologist. It was time for me to open my Center. Family and friends were not encouraging, they saw all the negatives and tried to discourage me, however, kept telling myself *"Yes I Can!" I can do this.*

Started my market research of the Countryside, Florida area. There was nothing available for learning disabled students. At the time, the parents had to wait two to three years to have their child evaluated by the school system. While waiting, the students were often labeled trouble makers.

There definitely was a market for my services. Who would buy these services? The numerous students being mislabeled by teachers as slow or trouble makers. My biggest problem was that I only had about $4,000.00 to start a business and also support my family. Needed to rent a place in a location where people had the finances to pay for testing and remedial work. A space with three or four rooms in this area cost about $600.00 a month, plus needed materials to work with the students. Finally found a place to rent where the owner had a son who needed testing and remedial work. We agreed on a six months barter deal, to include free rent, in exchange for diagnostic and remedial work with his son. Now had a place to start of my business.

Did I know anything about how to run a business? NO. Did I have a support system to encourage and give moral or financial support? NO. Did have the support of my two sons who liked to eat on a regular basis. They were very encouraging and helpful. I had more than ten years of experience working for a school system and private practice doing evaluations and remedial work with learning disabled students. With a lot of hard work and desire, I become *the* teacher, secretary, bookkeeper, public relations and marketing person, plus the cleaning lady. My Mother helped me out a few hours in the afternoon to answer the phone, which was a big help for me when I worked with students. For four months, until she went up north for the summer, Mom answered the phone and started "tea parties" for the students mothers as they waited for their children. That was a great success for everyone. I made many of the materials needed. Every spare opportunity I give free talks, visited doctors, psychologists, schools and told anyone who would listen all about the learning disabled person and what we were trained to do for the student at the *CENTER for LEARNING & DEVELOPMENT Inc.* I designed and made a brochure telling all about the *center* with our motto on the front, *"We Can because We Think We Can"*.

The motto is from my past. I was an average student at school, but my parents would get frequent calls from teachers telling them, " We know your daughter is smart enough however she has trouble reading and can't spell." My father worked with me, he taught me to think through the problems, he would say to me, *"yes, you can, let's figure out a way"*. Years later, in a university Special Education class, learned about learning disabilities. Yes, I am dyslexic, although prefer to say I have a learning problem. Still mix b and p and f and s, reverse numbers, read slow and my spelling is atrocious. It could be the result of my fractured scull and concussion from a bicycle accident when I was nine. I thank my father for his patience, he died February 1975.

Every piece of material that went out of the *center* was on light blue paper, even the test evaluations. The *center* became known as the *blue center,* it made us stand out. This was before people used colored paper. Everything was done on white paper back then. Anyone who worked with the student; doctors, teachers at their school, psychologists and parents received an evaluation. We all worked together as a team, to help the student progress. This also gave us good exposure, which led to further referrals. As we grew I hired new teachers and a speech therapist, Wendy.

A mother from the first five students was so pleased with the change in her son, she called the local newspaper, the *St. Petersburg Times*. What followed were two **unsolicited** articles with pictures by staff writers, the first by Carolyn Hopkins and the second by Peggy Peterman. There was a great response to both articles, which resulted in business growth.

We grew so fast the rental offices became too small for all the students. I was shown a property in the area, the owner offered to carry a mortgage. The house on the property was a dirty, filthy mess but the structure was good and I could see the potential. First had to hire a commercial group to empty the junk and do a general clean. Then my sons and I worked really hard to clean and paint the place. Next hired a carpenter to build shelves and room divides. Voila, we were ready for business at our "new" place.

before   **after**

The staff were all certified teachers and given extra training to teach the learning disabled. Also on the staff, a certified Psychologist Jackie, who assisted me with the evaluations and wrote the reports. After an evaluation, the teachers and myself discussed the expectations, each student had an individual program. The teachers where not to use labels like, dyslexic, ADD, ADHD and so on, who wants to live a life with a label. Yes, the students had learning problems but they could learn. The staff knew I had confidence in them and their abilities. If they needed help, was always available. We had monthly meetings to discuss each student, make changes if necessary and eat cookies. The students improved, many only needed a few months help after explaining to them the areas of difficulty and teaching them how to use their strengths to learn. The learning disabled person has strengths and weakness and is average or above in intelligence. The morale at the Center was great and everyone enjoyed working there. The waiting room and an empty walls had positive, encouraging, happy posters. We had a preschool in the mornings. With lots of work and the help of a wonderful staff the *Center* grew to a staff of twenty people.

As a woman owning a business let me share this story with you. People would call and ask to speak with the owner, when I got on the phone they said "no, no, we want to speak with *the man in charge."* So, would explain that I was the owner. After a while really got tired of this and decided to try something a little different. If I got the no, no, the man routine, would say "just a minute" wait a little bit and in the biggest voice I could muster say *"hello".* They either hung up or laughed and we did business.

Now well organized, could even play tennis one or two times a week. Playing tennis with many of my students parents was fun. This worked out to be good public relations and also a business expense.

As the *Center* grew so did the school system. The Director of the School System sent a notice to all their teachers telling them they were not to refer parents to the *CENTER for LEARNING & DEVELOPMENT...* because the school system now had more professionals working with the learning disabled and everything could be taken care of at the school, *at no cost*. Many teachers continued to refer, however it was becoming more difficult and we had less students. The *Center* added other services where there was a need, such as, extra math and preparation for the PSAT and SAT tests.

All was going pretty good and someone came along, offered me a price I could not afford to turn down for the property and preschool. After giving the students key training and sad good-byes, the Center for Learning & Development was closed. The new owners where not trained to teach Learning Disabilities, they intended to increase the size of the preschool.

What kind of business do you want to start? If I could do it, you can do it, remember to do your market research. My trust in *God*, faith in myself and hard work, it turned out better than I ever dreamed.

"Luck is where preparation meets opportunity" - Earl Nightingale

Time for dream two - what would that be?

Chapter Three

Dream Two Live and Work in a Foreign Country

I had worked long and hard, the buyers offer was substantial for the preschool business and property, God had seen me through these difficult times. Another dream was, *to live, work and experience another culture.*

The year was 1985, without any financial support both boys went to College on financial and job aid. Michael also had a scholastic scholarship. Both now educated young men, independent (they didn't *need* me anymore) and living on their own where they went to college.

My social life at this time was okay, had a few ventures in the dating world, they had not resulted in anything that was meaningful. A number of very nice men, however, could not imagine spending the rest of my life with any of them. On to my dreams.

So, how about the Peace Corps? Wish I had written down my sons comments when I told them what I wanted to do, somewhere between disbelief and hilarious. However, they decided *ooooookay,* they were my support system once again. Everyone else thought I was crazy. Why would a grown woman, who enjoyed some luxuries in life want to go in the Peace Corps?

Well, had no idea how difficult it was to become a Volunteer in the U.S. Peace Corps. After completing considerable paperwork, eight referrals, a trip to Atlanta for a seminar and a two hour phone interview, was finally accepted. After a few months wait, was asked if I would like to go to Tunisia. Not wanting to appear ignorant, (didn't know where Tunisia was) asked for 24 hours to make my decision. Called my sons with the location and asked if they knew anything about Tunisia. Then I went to the library. We found out as much as we could about Tunisia, in North Africa. It sounded like it would certainly be an interesting experience. *Interesting experience!!!* to say the least. Knew nothing about the Arab world or the Muslin religion and culture. Well, for that matter, didn't know much about any other culture.

After seeing my local doctor to complete medical forms, going back to my maiden name, good-bye parties with friends and long talks with both sons, off I went. A new group of 110 Peace Corps volunteers all met in Kansas City for three days of introductions, more paper work and the start of regular shots for everything, you can *not* even imagine. We then left for our plane journey to

Tunisia. Upon arrival we were taken for two days of R&R (rest and relaxation) at a tourist hotel. Oh boy, this was fun and then *culture shock*. We were then taken to our Tunisian apartments in Bertize for ten weeks of total culture submersion. The apartment shared with two other women, was a small two bedrooms with three foam mattresses, a very small kitchen with two electric burners, an office size refrigerator and a small bathroom. We walked one mile, four times a day, to the school. After lunch we went back to our apartment for a two hour rest. We sat on hard chairs for three meals and eight hours of language and culture classes. With temperatures in the 100 range during the days, we had no air conditioning, no comfortable chairs to sit on and intensive language training. After a week of this, perhaps my friends where right, maybe I was crazy. Was beginning to wonder about my decision. Oh well! lets see how it goes.

While in Betize, on hot nights the Tunisians would go up on their roof tops to catch some breeze. Someone had a *darbouka* (a drum), would started playing and out came their friends. They would sing until all hours. They certainly knew how to make the best of the hot nights.

Then came the Arab holiday, Ramadan, where the Muslin people fast all day and eat all night. Needless to say, during this period of time, work almost grinds to a halt. Then Aid Al Kabir, when we would see the children getting a sheep/lamb to take care of for about two weeks, this meant the animal went into the house. For the celebration, this same animal was slaughtered on the roof top by a person certified by the Mosque and the men in the family. Asked if I could observe this ritual, "yes, it was okay." Once was enough, you do not forget that experience, very bloody.

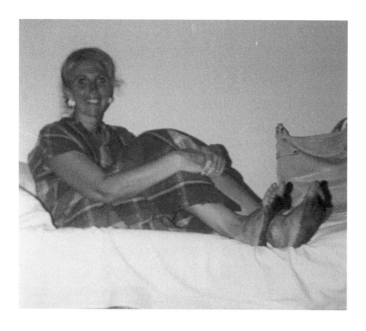

my feet

For weddings, the women decorated their hands and feet with decorative patterns using henna, a red/orange dye. To participate in the culture, let them talk me into decorating my feet. Just picture these big, size 10 feet with an orange/black pattern on then. A sight to behold, words cannot describe so here is a picture.

Shortly after this, about six weeks into training, we sat talking while waiting for the teacher. Out of nowhere, I got a severe head ache. It felt like someone hit me in the back of my head with an ax. I burst out crying, not something I would normally do, but the pain was excruciating. After a week of stronger and stronger medicine and one day sleeping for almost 24 hours, there was still no relief. The doctor at the Embassy decided to tell me I had a brain tumor and would be leaving for Washington, DC in the morning. Arrived in Washington on Friday. Peace Corps had set up a neurologist appointment for me. My son, Michael in Boston, was informed and had flown in to be with me. We started with the exam and then the doctor looked at to my feet. Well, in all the pain had forgotten about my feet. The doctor looked horrified. He was sure I have some unknown horrible disease. I couldn't help but burst out laughing. My son who was sitting in the office heard me laughing. Guess Michael was sure I probably had cracked under the strain and started banging on the door. "Everything okay?" The doctor let him in the room. They both sat there while I explained about my feet. It was now too late for a cat scan, so we had to try to get though the weekend without the next appointment. Michael was trying so hard to do anything he could to make it easier while the pain persisted. However, by Monday the pain was not quite as bad. The cat scan done in the morning didn't show a tumor So, what was causing this pain? After talking with another doctor and a counselor, they decided, what I had was a very severe allergic reaction to the *harissa*, a spice, put in the food at every meal. It also explained why after three days of eating western food the headache was disappearing. You just never know! Was very thankful it wasn't what the Embassy doctor thought. So, back to Tunisia for the last week of training, my diet was now restricted to plain food and crackers.

At this time, let me share some of my first impressions and information from our cultural sessions. Women were told not to go out at night without a male escort. Two Peace Corps women did not heed the warning and were beaten at a train station one night. There seemed to be garbage everywhere. Asked about this and was told that many of the uneducated felt it was a freedom to just drop paper, etc. wherever they wanted. The school classrooms often had 40 students in a class, but discipline was not a problem. As a child progressed and showed ability, they were moved on. Many of the educated spoke four languages, Tunisian Arabic, Classical Arabic, French and English. As a people, they were not very friendly, however after they got to know you and trust you, they became wonderful friends. They were very family oriented, older women did not go out to public party places, but did attend social parties at their friends homes. The married woman was expected to be home when the children were there. Married women socialize at the *hamum*, (a large sauna) the gossip center. The women over 40 wore a *sofsari*, which looked like a sheet that wraps around you and they held one end in their mouth. The younger women wore western clothes. For me, because I was older, a trench coat proved to be helpful, although very hot in the summer. One observation that really surprised me, on Sundays, you often saw the men out walking or playing with their children. Because of the French influence on Tunisia they mostly followed our work week, except Friday afternoons they went to the Mosque, Moslem temple. Some worked Saturday mornings.

We had now been assigned to our job sites. Mine was in the city of Tunis, just outside the medina (walled city). Peace Corps does not help you find a place to live, if you were placed out in the countryside, it was easier, the monthly stipend went a long way. However, if you were in the city, it's almost impossible to find a place to live. It took six weeks to find a place in La Kram, 45 minutes out of Tunis by train. Before finding this place stayed with five other Peace Corps people who could not find a place either. All we could find with the money we had was in a seedy hotel. It was not unusual at this hotel, to see Tunisian men expose themselves. We never walked anywhere in the hotel alone.

By the way, the drop-out rate for Peace Corps Volunteers (PCV's) in Tunisia at the time was about 50%.

My Peace Corps job was to work with four Tunisian deaf women and one hearing woman who took the phone calls and set the appointments. The volunteer before me had written a grant for sewing machines, however she had no ideas how to develop this business. The women could sew with the skills of a couture seamstress. After watching the women and the volunteer who would be leaving in a month, decided to make a number of changes.

women seamstresses

First of all, the deaf women did not realize this was their very own business, they thought it was for the Peace Corps. With the help of a Tunisian tutor, Mohammed, we explained it was *their business.* There was a big smile and then the work began. I felt it was important to teach them about money and work ethics, they already knew how to sew. They had very few customers, the average Tunisian could not afford custom made cloths. Their friends would come to sit all day long and "talk" with the deaf women. They had been paid for this by the previous PCV with money left from her grant. Where were the women who could afford this couture sewing? These women were very talented, if the customer took their piece of cloth, describe what they wanted, the women could make it. After researching the community, found out there was an Organization of International Women who met once a month for a meeting. I spoke with the president of the organization and told her about the women. She said yes, they could model at the next meeting. My plan was in motion. We took the deaf women into the medina to buy fabric, Mohammed did the bargaining. Now each woman was to make herself a beautiful outfit, which they did. US AID (United States Aid Organization) was about two blocks away. I went and spoke with people there, they loaned me a car and driver for a few hours to take the women to this meeting. I taught them how to model their outfits, gave each a number with hand signals. As they modeled, I talked about the women and their skills . It was wonderful to see them smile as they modeled. The response was huge, we had more business then they could initially handle. Their business was off and running.

September 26, 1985, shortly after arriving at my job site that day, there was a bang, ten minutes later a bigger bang. Opened the porch door, another bomb exploded, we could smell something strange. Immediately called the Embassy, was told someone was sending letter bombs in the area. They suspected Libya, one person was already hurt badly. A crowd gathered, the police chased them away using clubs. The women were very scared, so decided to get them out and send them home. Just as we left the building the police dispersed the crowd again and we were almost trampled. It was extremely frightening.

During this time, I was still living at *that* hotel, received a call from a Embassy person. She was going out of the country and needed someone to house sit and take care of her animals. Boy! didn't know I could say yes so fast. The lady's house I'm staying at was the Press Attaché for our Embassy, her home had all the creature comforts, what a wonderful treat. October 1, 1985, Israel bombed the PLO head quarters in Hamma Chatt, Tunis. The phone began ringing. Now, you need to know, Peace Corps volunteers are not to be political and this volunteer was pretty ignorant anyway. It was a circus. The Tunisians blamed the United States, so we were put on alert, told to lay low and be ready to evacuate. There were daily demonstrations in Tunis. A tank was positioned outside our Embassy, this did cause concern for all Americans. Eventually it did quiet down. Yes, I went from being a rather quiet, divorced woman and mother, into this hot seat of political turmoil.

Finally moved into what would be my PC home. It was across a lake from the bombed PLO headquarters, you could see it from my roof top. Where I lived made friends with many Tunisians, could not have survived without them. They helped me in numerous ways, especially getting my big gas bottles up to my apartment. On occasion a group of Tunisian would visit, wine tucked under their jackets. Yes, they did drink wine in private. We would then sit, drink wine and eat cheese and checkers that I provided. We discussed our cultures and the differences, this was very informative. There was much the Peace Corps did not teach and the eye did not see. One

of the helpers, a Tunisian doctor, Mondher, became a good friend during that time. I did not find out the correct pronunciation for some time and always called him "mother." It was a little joke with his friends until they helped me with the correct pronunciation. Mondher introduced me to his family. His mother invited me to afternoon tea. Until the Arab spring we corresponded, I have not been able to get in touch with *my* La Kram family since then. Needless to say, I am concerned.

tea with Mondhers family

It's hard to explain the layout of my apartment, perhaps my son's comment when he came to visit will explain. Chip, my older son, looked in the door, stood there with a grin and said "nice high ceilings, where do I stay?" He stayed there with me. There was a bedroom, living room with a small three feet by two feet box with a door that opened into the living room and a kitchen with a sink and two burners. The small room was the bathroom, with a toilet, sink and shower. You could do all while standing in the same spot. It made the training apartment look great. I talked with the *Assess*, he was the man who stood at the front door of this old, in need of repair building with five apartments. He would let me use the outside table and chairs. A straw bed and another bed, all had been stored away for the winter season. My son got the bedroom, I took the straw bed in the living room, such creature comfort! In the winter, it was cold and damp, causing constant changing wall decorations, thanks to the mildew. Here is a picture of my son and myself standing in front of a Tunisian carpet, it was there to cover a big crack in the wall.

Chip and me in front of the carpet

The evening after he arrived I had a cocktail party for everyone to meet my son. My Tunisian friend Mondhers' mom made us a variety of delicious food. The drinks flowed and so did the people, trying to find a place to sit.

Received permission to rent a car for my his visit. This allowed us to tour Tunisia. Mondher had helped me plot a circle tour on a map and checked to make sure there would be hotels. Time was limited, so the next day, off we went into the desert. It had a beautiful oasis. Then on to the homes built into the hills, that's where we stayed overnight. It was there that parts of Star Wars was filmed. Next day continued on to Jerba, we spent a day and night at the beach. On the way back to Tunis, we stopped at a large medina for us to do some gift shopping before he returned home. It was so nice to see him, time went too fast.

It was suggested I take a French class because they found a French book for the deaf with hand signs. So went to school at the French Cultural Society. One of the young men in class invited my to his Grandmother's *Dar Arby* (home) for lunch. It was a home built during the Ottoman period, 16th -17th century, with the original dirt floors, a center court yard with many small rooms off the center. After we washed our hand from a bucket of water, the Grandmother served a wonderful Tunisian meal, consisting of *tagine, brique*, and *swabaa fatma*. The young man and I sat in a separate room. Everything was going fine, very interesting and educational, until he retrieved a boom box to play American music. He said he wanted to make me comfortable. Had him put it away immediately, talk about ruining the ambiance.

On April 15, 1986, the United States bombed Libya. Once again we were on ready alert. This time two friends and myself got permission to go to Morocco for a week. Morocco, at the time, was more modern than Tunisia. The men and women both wore a long robe called a *Jellaba* on the street. They looked very neat and appeared more friendly. Did notice there were more military people standing around. After shopping at the medina in Casablanca, we were treated first to drinks at the famous bar, Rick's Cafe bar and then to dinner. This was a treat from a man we met previously on the plane that day during our flight from Tunis. The next day we took a train from Casablanca to Marrakech, where there was a big open area with snake charmers, belly dancers, etc. That evening we enjoyed a beautiful cultural display called Fantasia. We then rented a car with a driver and were driven on to Fez, with it's a huge medina. There, we saw a beautiful Mosque and numerous small shops. We were all fascinated at one place where we observed people dying leather.

dye pots

The next day we continued by bus to Rabat, the capital of Morocco. While there we stopped at our Embassy to report our schedule of departure and get the latest news about Tunis. We continued by bus to Casablanca, then flew back to Tunisia.

While staying at the Press Attaché house for that hectic week, I met another Embassy person who lived across the street. She was a young woman who said I'd make a nice substitute mom, she asked me how I would feel about that. Felt it was a nice compliment and said "sure, talk with me any time." As time passed we would meet for lunch. At one of those meetings met her colleague form the Venezuelan Embassy. He decided that I should meet his Ambassador, a private lunch was arranged. The best dress I had with me to wear for the occasion was a plain knit dress I purchased for $9.99 on sale before leaving the states. Upon arrival the maid went to take my coat and there it was, a spot right in the front of my dress. As I went to shake hands with the Ambassador, put my left hand over the spot. It was evident he had noticed because he laughed, we became friends. As a result of this meeting, he and his lady friend included me on different occasions at their dinner parties. It was a very interesting experience to be at these functions. Among other things, the food was great! I didn't realize that most or all of the other guests where communist country Ambassadors, I was the only American at these dinners. So during the day I was pushed and squeezed on public transportation. On the occasion of the dinners, the Ambassador's driver would pick me up at my apartment to take me to the Ambassadors residence. These were strictly social functions, it was interesting to discuss world affairs and the culture of the different countries. Most of the time they would speak English, occasionally French. Although my ability to speak French was poor, did understand more than they thought but I did not respond. Definitely got the impression that Americans are thought of as being loud and always telling people what to do. On one occasion, at my table was the Ambassador from Cuba and his wife, Ambassador from Poland and his wife and a Tunisian Ambassador to Bahrain, whom I would date when he was in Tunis. One weekend the Venezuelan Ambassador's girlfriend was out of town, he contacted me and asked if I would like to join him for brunch on Sunday. After brunch we took a walk on the beach. During our casual conversation asked him why he decided to invite me to his dinners. He said, "because you are not impressed with anything. You're just relaxed and enjoy the evening." It was a very educational and interesting experience to be a part of the many societies in Tunisia. About a month before departing Peace Corps, found out that I was being investigated by our Embassy because I was the only American invited to this Ambassadors social functions. Maybe I missed my calling, an *International spy!*

Grocery shopping was a daily experience, did not have a refrigerator. After getting off the train on my way home would stop to buy vegetables in a converted garage. It usually took about an hour, the venders would teach me the Arabic name and I taught them the English name for the fruit or vegetables. They were usually waiting for me, it was always fun,

There was always something going on, the Expat community had many activities which I was often invited to, most of the PCV's were under 30 years of age or over 60, I was neither. My friend, Mondher, who had a small green car, would come pick me up and off we'd go to the parties. We both liked to dance, he was a great dancer.

What would the first Christmas away from my children be like for them and me? They assured me they would be fine, they had friends. They were really great to me during my time in Tunisia, both sent me "care packages" on a regular basis. Well, let me assure you, holidays overseas the ExPats look after one another. Was offered to house sit at an Embassy home in Sidi Bou Said. Ever night between Christmas and New Years we had a party with everyone, Tunisians, Americans, etc., and everyone brought something. It was great fun. One sad thing during the stay, witnessed a Tunisian funeral, which went right past the home.

During my stay in Tunis was invited to fly in a Glider plane. What an exciting adventure. Once the glider was cut loose from the pull plane all you heard was a low whistling sound. The glider flew close to the mountain to pick up an air current. I kept yelling to the pilot "we're close enough, could see the ants on the hill." My seat was in front of the glider. Was a little nervous about landing, but it landed smooth on the grass. Was also invited to go sailing on the Mediterranean with friends, the azure waters were beautiful until all of a sudden, a storm came up. Fortunately, the boat owner was a great captain, we returned to shore without a problem.

While working in Tunis you are to get a "Carte de Sejouru" permit, or go out of the country for a weekend every three months. I choose to go out every three months. One trip was to Malta, a quaint island in the Mediterranean sea. Landing was an interesting experience. As the pilot made his descent through the clouds, oh! no Malta. Soon felt the lift of the plane as we do a quick climb back up into the clouds. The second try, hurray! there's Malta, everyone on the plane clapped. Was told the pilots were learning how to read instruments but were still flying by what they could see. Malta was a very interesting place with its old buildings, narrow winding streets, colorfully painted fishing boats, language a mixture of Arabic, Italian and English. Got very brave and took a bus out to the countryside to see, what they called, a small Stone Hedge. It's a group of large stones found at the end of the island. The bus ride was quite an experience, wondered if I would ever get back to the capital. Eventually did, then returned to Tunis.

On a long weekends, two other women and myself went down to Jerba. Jerba is a holiday spot for the Germans tourists, who swim topless. So, here we are down at the beach and two helicopters fly over very low with guns drawn. We realize it was Libya, who the U.S. had recently bombed. We definitely stood out as Americans with our tops up, so what to do? If we pulled our tops down we would be very white, so we dove on the beach, face down. It was never dull!

June 17, 1986 was medivaced again, this time for knee surgery after a fall. Was advised by the doctor not to return to Tunisia. Did anyway at the end of July, to find the third Peace Corps Director. I was called to her office and greeted with "everybody knows you" and said I could no longer deal with the Expats. She did not understand, nor did she seem interested to know, they where the people supporting the Peace Corps sewing project. Decided not to stay, my knee was swelling and would need surgery again. Took four months to organize the deaf women, review with them different business procedures and say my good-byes. Found out later this third Director only stayed about six months.

Went to visit my Tunisian family, Mondher told me he would be moving to Paris to further his education. A few years later when I visited Paris, stayed with him and his French wife at their apartment which had a view of the Eiffel Towel. How's that for lucky!

Also visited Mohammed, my tutor, he married a Dutch lady and moved to Holland. Had visited them in Holland, he has visited me in Florida with his Dutch wife and two young sons.

Before returning home from Tunis, the couple who's house I stayed at in Sidi Bou Said, were transferred to Egypt. They invited me to visit before returning home. Bad knee and all, off I went to Egypt.

For me, do not have the words to describe or explain Egypt, it was more then I could assimilate. To look at the pyramids and then think of when they were build. Sakkara, the oldest stone building built 2686 BC. How had they accomplished that? Took a cruise up the Nile with an Egyptologist on the ship, he brought everything to life, including the hieroglyphics, from Luxor to Aswan. Temple of Luxor, Karnak with a light and sound show, Ramsis the Great, Valley of the Kings, with many tombs including Tutankhamen, King Tut. Took a boat ride on the feluccas, a small sail boat, then to botanical gardens. The last stop on the cruise, Abu Simbel, Ramsis II at the Aswan High Dam. What a trip! so much to see and try to comprehend. Bussed back to Cairo, it's an experience just to see how they navigated the crowded roads. Went to the Egyptian Museum in Cairo, to see the wealth found in King Tut's tomb, unbelievable. Also went to a few private parties with Egyptians in their beautiful saris. Such an interesting culture, although their class systems did bother me.

Shortly before leaving, my friends were invited to the Suez Canal for short cruise on the U.S.Missouri. They said I could go on the bus trip with them, then wait in town for a few hours.

All the invited guests were dressed "to the nines" for this special occasion. They suggested I dress down to walk around the port town. On the bus trip, the person in charge decided at the last minute it was to dangerous for me to be left alone in town. Was instructed to board the tender, which was taking everyone to the U.S.Missouri. So, last one on, was first one off, up I go, through the color guard and receiving line. When I got to the commander, felt the need to say something because of my casual attire. I greeted him with "Sir, I've come to crash your party". He laughed, we explained, he assigned a sailor to be my escort and he gave me a complete, private tour of the ship. I did see the plaque showing where the signing took place at the end of World War II.

My time in the Peace Corps was more than I expected it would be, it was beyond any expectations. What an amazing learning experience. It opened up new worlds for me and changed my life and way of thinking. Thank you God.

P.S. Recently learned that the Peace Corps application process is shorter and quicker now. Would this or something like this interest you?

"The best way to get a good idea is to get a lot of ideas."

- Linus Pauling, Nobel Prize winning chemist

Chapter Four

What next ?

So here I am back in Florida to have the second knee surgery with a doctor who does nothing but knee surgery. I watched the surgery on a video screen. After physical therapy, Mom and I moved to the Indian Rocks condo.

When I returned from Peace Corps my sister asked if my Mom could live with me six months and then she would live with her the other six months. It's your Mom, you say okay. I had a new condo on Indian Rocks beach, we had each contributed to buy some new furniture. My sister had bought a new home but no room for Mom. So instead of six months, Mom moved in full time with me.

So what next *the world!* The little that I had seen was just enough to whet my appetite, there was so much more to learn about and see. As usual with me, didn't know how I'd do this but there must be away. Determined to figure it out, I asked *God* for help.

Started by going to every seminar could find on international business and took jobs that would teach me more marketing and selling skills. Then began reading books on the countries I wanted to go to. Australia, Singapore, Peoples Republic of China (PRC), Thailand and India, their various customs and ways of doing business. Noticed they all wanted or needed medical products. With all my book read country knowledge and numerous seminars, I then began talking with people doing international business and started to put together a plan. This process took a little more than two years.

The Plan - started an Export Management Company. The Center for Learning and Development Corporation was now doing business as TAM International Trading Company, Inc. Began talking with small to midsize medical companies around my area who were doing business in the United States. Then made appointments with them to see if they were interested in marketing their products overseas. The Plan was to represent a number of companies and develop distributorships for them in the above mentioned countries.

After much discussion, haggling over commissions and learning the product lines, got ready for my first business trip. The companies were to give me samples and the marketing materials we selected. My son, Chip came down and took me to the airport to see me off on my new adventure. Right down to the last minute, on the way, we stopped at the last company I had recruited, who finally had their samples and marketing materials ready.

Now, you need to realize, I was so excited about actually taking a trip around the world by myself that there were many business areas that should've been done differently but ... off I went, "in *God's* hands".

+++++++++

March 30th, 1989 Departed on my first business trip, with the help of many friends from my Peace Corps experience, had places to stay along the way. Decided that Tunisia, North Africa would be my first stop. A friend who was currently in Ireland gave me his place to stay. It was a joy to once again see the deaf women who were still sewing and they were doing the project on their own. They were no longer a Peace Corps project. Called on a number of medical companies and visited with many old friends.

April 10th arrived in Bombay, India on a plane that landed at midnight. An airport policeman looked at the address I gave him, banged on a parked taxi cab to wake the driver, said something and off we went. After a half-hour of driving and seeing people sleeping on the side of the streets in a residential areas, the driver stopped and told me "get out." All the homes had gates around them, I was scared but knew India had a caste system, figured staying in the taxi cab would probably be safe. In the very firm voice, said, "No, you get out." So, here I sat in the back of the cab, it was now about 1: a.m., as I looked around, really didn't know what to do. Just sat there hoping a car or the police would come along. Nothing! After about 15 minutes the driver came back, got in the cab and drove off. Where was he taking me now? Soon, we drove up to an apartment complex with a guard in front, the driver stopped and said *"here."* It was now about 1:30 in the morning, asked the guard if my friends lived here. He said yes, and carried my bag to their apartment. We knocked and rang the bell. After ten very long minutes, Mike opened the door and looked stunned. Mike and Eve Marie, were transferred from Cairo, Egypt. He finally invited me into their apartment. He knew I was coming but did not know when. After being there a week, my letter finally arrived, telling him when to expect me. Was very thankful they were home when I did arrive and they let me stay.

Had been corresponding with a foreign service national (FSN) gentleman, Srinivas, from the commercial department of the U.S. Embassy in India. He had arranged meetings for me with several medical companies. After many days and numerous business calls the prospects were beginning to look more promising. It was very helpful for me being able to stay with old friends at the end of very hectic, trying business days.

In Bombay when a taxi stopped at the corner for a light, oftentimes a deformed hand would be pushed in the window begging. No matter how warm, my window was always closed. If you walked slowly to look around, children would surround you in the street begging. Bombay (now Mumbai) is the business center for India. It was dirty and crowded with many beggars and a caste system which was difficult to overlook. Wound up with four possible business prospects and two commitments, which I faxed to the companies before leaving.

Did meet some very interesting people in Bombay. One was a woman, Sarita, who wanted me to represent her products. She was trying to preserve the Art products produced by the master craftsmen of India. She invited me to dinner with her family, to show me the products. Upon arriving was informed the father would not be eating with us so it was mother, sister, Sarita and myself. They were considered an upper middle-class family. We sat on the floor and the women ate with their hands, guess this was the custom but it did surprise me.

April 25th left for Delhi and then to Nepal to visit my friend, however it was not to be that simple. The plane was to depart at 9:45 a.m.. At 9:30 we where all taken to breakfast at the airport cafeteria. It was hot, the air conditioning was not working and we saw our plane being towed away from the terminal. About two hours passed before we were told to go back and reclaim our luggage. Turned out I was aboard a Russian plane going to Moscow with a stop in Delhi. My bags were opened and very carefully checked. I had thrown a candy tasting diet aid in my cosmetic bag which created much concern. Thank goodness it tasted like candy. Two of the inspectors had to taste them. By this time, the Indian business people I had been sitting with at breakfast came over to see if they could help and my bags were soon closed. At that point, we found out there was a Russian diplomat family on board and we had a bomb threat. Finally boarded a plane about 3: p.m.. Upon boarding we saw the diplomat family. Then I remembered having seen them quickly escorted away when we where originally waiting to board earlier that morning.

After spending all day waiting with everyone, when we arrived in Delhi, one of the men who was staying overnight at the same hotel offered to share a taxi. Later he called and invited me to join him for a drink in his room then we'd go out to dinner. He seemed nice enough so said okay. While we were sitting having a drink, he excused himself for a minute and came back with cocaine. Needless to say, I bolted out of that room. The worst thing that could happen was to be caught in a foreign country with drugs. What a day!

The next morning was so glad to see my friend Barbara, from the Embassy, at the Kathmandu airport. Slept most of the day, was rather stressed out from yesterday's ordeal. At that time there were very few cars on the road because India had cut off the supply of gas to Nepal. The people were kind and gentle, with many intriguing customs, religious ceremonies and fascinating buildings. One day Barbara decided to take me to a religious building beside the Ganges. We were on the roof of the building when we started to sense a strange smell. As we looked over Barbara informed me they were having a cremation. It is a smell and sight I will never forget. Three bodies were being burned, one was obviously a child. After this ceremony, the ashes are then put into the river Ganges, which at that time of the year was not much more than a small stream.

On another day, Barbara took me to the American Club, where I met a man who was with SEVA, a blindness prevention organization. He worked with a doctor in India who would benefit with an Interocular Lens lab. One of my medical companies made this lab. What a lucky introduction. This turned out to be one of my most successful business leads. If this deal goes through, my trip would be paid. The Lab people and SEVA joined partners. Trip paid!

Actually went to Nepal just to visit my friend and it turned out to also be the start of a very successful small import business for about five years. Discovered some of the most beautiful jewelry and other interesting products that would sell very well in Florida area boutiques where I lived.

While in Nepal took a few days to fly into Chitwan National Park, where I stayed at the TreeTops hotel. Went on an elephant safari, saw many rhinoceros and other animals, one evening a tiger. This was in the Himalayas, saw the impressive Mt Everest, a look at *God's* creations, breathtaking.

May 11th arrived in beautiful, clean, modern and safe Singapore, then took a taxi to Larry's home, another Embassy friend from my time in the Peace Corps. I had caught a bad cold, so spent most of the day at his home setting up my appointments for Monday morning. Larry and his girlfriend decided some time at the beach would be good for my cold. We went to Johor, Malaysia and some fun in the sun. It felt wonderful to be on beautiful beaches and eat delicious fresh fruit. Was ready for the clients on Monday. Made some contacts. One medical company seemed interested in a few of the products, so I left samples and information. They had a lot of questions, which made me realize this company had not given me enough training.

May 28th on to Hong Kong, where to simply land between the buildings and water was an accomplishment for the pilots, they now have a new airport. Many of my appointments met me at the hotel where I stayed. Thursday afternoon called the embassy to check if it was okay to go into Beijing, they said yes. Decided to go two days early, the medical conference I was scheduled to attend did not start until Monday.

Arrived about 4: p.m. Friday afternoon, passed right through customs. A young man asked if I needed a taxi. He took my bags, we exchanged some money and into a van. A man was already waiting in the van, Alan, from England. He had been doing business in China for about five years. We exchanged business cards, he told me if I had any questions to call him. He stayed at the Great Wall Hotel, a few blocks from the Kunlun Hotel where I stayed.

After settling in the hotel, looked out the window, what a sight, hundreds of bicycles speeding along plus cabs and buses waiting outside the hotel. It was now around 5:30 p.m., decided to wait till the following day to start sightseeing and went down to dinner. There were many groups of people, I appeared to be the only person sitting by myself. After dinner phoned Jeff, a person Larry told me was also in the U.S. Embassy in Tunis. He remembered me and invited me to brunch on Sunday.

June 3rd, 1989, got up and went go down for breakfast, then to the front desk and asked for a cab. Was told we could not go out, there was trouble. Went back up to my room and looked out the window, there were no bicycles or busses on the road. Phoned Alan, he informed me he was just leaving for Tiananmen Square. He came around and picked me up. We saw very little traffic on the road, no bikes. We went into Tiananmen Square. All the speakers were blasting out something in Chinese. As we started walking around the square, we stopped and ask if anyone spoke English. Within seconds we had a crowd around us. They told us the troops were coming and everyone was to get out of the Square. We moved on, decided to take a picture of each other in front of *their* Statue of Liberty.

standing by Statue

Again we asked the students and were told the same thing. Allen was sure nothing would happen however I was getting a little nervous. As I looked around, we appeared to be the only Caucasians in the area. Luckily, the taxi driver waited for us. We got back in the taxi and headed out when a man with a make-believe gun signals to us to turn around, the driver argued then turned. We were temporarily stopped by crowds of people surrounding two army trucks with soldiers. Hiding on the floor of the taxi, stuck my camera up to take pictures. Finally got up and looked, we were surrounded by soldiers everywhere and waved forward.

Back at the hotel, turned on the TV. There it was, all the troops coming into the square. Called Jeff, the man from the embassy. He said it was true and try to get out any way I could. The government could not help, I was there as a private citizen. Quickly placed a call to the travel agent in Hong Kong, he said he would try to do something. Then, sat glued to the TV, not believing my eyes as I saw people running to get out of the square. Their Statue of Liberty was already torn down. When I went to dinner, tried to talk with some of the American groups, everyone was in a panic. Decided to go down to the little store, to buy some food products. Then tried to call someone in my family but all the phone lines were tied up. There wasn't anything else I could do so went to bed, hoping when I woke up it would be all over.

Sunday, got up, turned on the TV, the situation was very tense. Was not allowed to go out of the hotel. Tanks and troops were everywhere shooting and killing. The roads were empty. Decided to go down to lunch, the waiters asked me what group I was with. Told them, I'm by myself. Was told they were only feeding the groups. One group had me join them for lunch. At dinnertime the restaurant stopped me and said I could not sit with the group because food was running short. Went back to the little store to buy more food, it was closed. In my room, tried room service, sorry. Thank goodness I had bought stuff the other day.

Monday, the travel agent did get through on the phone and said he could get me out next Saturday. This would be great for a diet, however there must be something I could do. The hotel stopped TV coverage, so didn't even know what was happening. The floor bellboy was no longer there with his friendly smile. Went down to the lobby to talk and try to find out any news. Called Alan, he could not help me. He kept telling me not to worry.

Tuesday, was told that over at the Great Wall Hotel there was a ticket agent. Tried to get someone to walk over with me but no one would. *I was definitely on my own.* I was petrified, made sure my white hair and face were showing as I walked over to the hotel. There was no one on the streets but a few soldiers who just looked at me. At the hotel there were big lines. After an hour or so, finally got to an agent. Could get a confirmed ticket for Saturday, the one the Hong Kong agent made for me, started to walk away. The person behind me said take it, just in case, so I did. When I got back to the hotel, the people looked at me surprised. All the groups were being bused to the airport. No, I could not get on their bus. By the time I returned to my room, was getting really nervous. Started praying and the phone rang. It was Jeff, "get yourself to the airport as quick as possible, anyway you can. There is a United Airlines flight coming in and it will take people, if they are not full." It was about 11:15 a.m., laid my clothes around the room and rang for the bellboy. When he came to the door, motioned to all the clothes and told him the clothes were for him, needed a taxi to the airport. He told me, "no taxi". Once again, motioned to everything in the room, pointed to him and said American dollars to the airport. He left the room. I finished getting ready and prayed again. Ten minutes later, the bellboy was back, takes everything, he brought me down to two young men who had a car. Off we go, they kept pointing to all the tanks, troops and guns along the way. When we arrived at the airport, it was a madhouse. They let me off at the local entrance, I needed International. People pointed the way, saw a United Airlines stand, the man behind was stepping down. Frantically, I yell, he stopped and asked, "how many"? One "OK, yes, your charge card," I was on my way. Two more people came behind me but the plane was full and they could not get on, felt sorry for them. As the plane took off, everybody let out a cheer. Free drinks were passed to everyone.

Didn't care where they were going, just out of Beijing, we went to Japan. Missed a connection to LA by about a half hour so stayed overnight. Was able to contact my family, told them what happened, where I was, would leave for the U.S. tomorrow morning.

About a month after I was home, my neighbor noticed I was not going out of my condo. It took about two weeks for the drama and stress of the situation to really hit me. Everyone just kept saying, "boy, what an adventure, you where part of history".

And so ended my first international business trip as, Tam International Trading Company, didn't think it was supposed to be like this. I was very thankful, *God* certainly was with me.

Okay, not everyone wants to experience other countries and learn their cultures. Should I, will I, continue with this business venture?

"Courage is the ability to go from failure to failure without losing enthusiasm."

- Winston Churchill

Chapter Five

More Trips and New Countries

Yes, I will continue this business idea. So, after returning from a trip my time was spent with follow-up faxes, checking up on medical sales and more education on medical products. Started selling the imports from Nepal. Friends asked if they could have home parties so they would have the first chance to buy these imports; jewelry, unique jackets and pants, small leather goods. It was a good suggestion, this gave me an idea of what would sell in the boutiques. So, in the future, upon arriving home, someone had a home party. They wanted to buy everything however, needed samples to show. We worked out this problem, I took their orders also.

During my time home, was invited to join Rotary International, which I did.

* * * *

Trip Two March 6, 1990

First stop was Paris, France to visit some friends. On March 11th travelled on to Tunis, Tunisia to check on companies that I had called on last year, visited some friends and check on the Peace Corps project. The ladies were surprised and happy to see me again, the project was still succeeding, yea! Medical sales did not look promising in Tunis so returned to Paris on the 19th, for more visiting and sightseeing.

On my trips, I brought along Rotary flags from my chapter. When I went to Rotary meetings in various countries, we exchanged flags. Back then most of the international groups were all men. Surprised to see a woman, they would question why I was at their meeting. Upon showing them my pin and card, with a friendly smile, they invited me to join them. They wanted to know why I was in their country. Told them to sell medical products from the medical companies I represented and was also interested in buying unique handmade products from their country. By the end of the meetings, the Rotarians had contact names for me. Also got to meet some very nice local people.

March 24th Bombay, India via Frankfurt, Germany. We sat on the runway waiting for clearance to fly. The Captain finally came on the speaker and said "something is happening somewhere over

Syria, Egypt or Poland, we have been denied flying space." The plane returned to the airport. Three hours later we left, with no explanation except "we now have a route to fly." In Bombay, followed up on medical leads and made some small sales. Found more interesting imports; beautiful writing paper and a larger variety of leather goods which I knew would sell.

March 29th Bangkok, Thailand decided to attend a meeting of Rotary International, once again, all men. The men were cordial as I took a seat at one of the large round tables. We were all given an envelop from the speaker when we entered the room. Decided to check what was in the envelope so emptied it onto the table. Out fell reading material and several condoms. Realized everyone at the table was staring at me, my face turned red, they burst out laughing. They knew the speaker was the man who went into the countryside teaching the native population about HIV. That night there was a knock on my door at the Royal Orchid Hotel, where I was staying. The manager of the hotel was at my table during the meeting, he sent me a note with a gift, a very nice robe with the hotels insignia. It re-affirmed my belief that people everywhere in the world can be kind and fun to be with.

The following day contacted some medical companies. Also found and bought some beautiful Thai silk jackets to sell back home.

April 3rd, Singapore, made followup calls and answered more medical questions but no business deals. However was taken to dinner by two of the prospective clients, which I thought was very nice.

April 10th, Hong Kong, follow up calls, again no business. Hopped on a bus for a beautiful ride through the countryside to the Stanley Market. While there found some great products to sell.

April 17th, Melbourne, Australia, some very promising medical leads. Also found more imports that would sell . Flew up to Sydney, saw the beautiful Opera House, the area surrounding it that has a wide variety of fun activities. At the Rotary meeting, was given a contact person who ordered some imports from Nepal.

April 22nd, arrived back home.

* * * *

Trip Three January 7, 1991

Left Tampa, Florida, for Sydney, Australia. Was met by a contact from my trip last year and taken to an apartment in Manly which had a beautiful view of the harbor. He also took me out for a delicious fish dinner. In the morning, hopped on the ferry into Sidney. What a great way to start a day. Met with contacts from last year, then was taken to the American Club for lunch. The next day attended a Rotary meeting. At both places many people gave me contacts to meet which included both medical companies and people who had unique products. Sidney was a great city, with much to see and do. The people were friendly and it had a good transportation system. Then down to Melbourne and followed up with contacts from last year. All very nice but still no sales.

January 17th, arrived in Hong Kong. Met with contacts and acquired a small order from one medical company. On the 19th went to Stanley market again and found more unique gifts. Then took the Tram up The Peak, which was very exciting and had a beautiful view. You could see the colorful boat people in the harbor and the unique architecture of the buildings in Hong Kong. On the 22nd took a wonderful one day boat trip to Guangzhou.

January 26th, arrived in a new country, Indonesia. In Jakarta went to a Rotary meeting to get help with contacts. At one of the contact companies, the owner was having a birthday party for her mother that night and extended an invitation to me. The mother's gift was a karaoke machine, it was lots of fun. They were going away for the weekend, she offered her driver. He picked me up at the hotel and gave me a city tour on Saturday. There is nothing nicer than having a local person show you the city, it was wonderful. Found some lovely jewelry to import. That evening the hotel took the guests to a production of Ethnic Music and Dance. The performers were in native dress to dance and sing, it was beautiful. The band used all instruments made of bamboo. After the show, we each received one of the unique bamboo musical instruments as a gift. It now hangs on my living room wall and reminds me how enriched my life has been through travel. So glad I had the courage to act on my dreams.

At the production met a man from National Geographic, who said I should consider going to Bali. A new Hilton was opening, rooms would be half price. Told him, would think about it. Decided to go, it was very warm, so went down to the pool for a swim. While approaching the pool heard a person say, "Hi Teri," it was the man from National Geographic. He knew Bali and suggested places to see during the day. Evenings would join him for drinks and sing-alongs, lots of fun, it was a nice break. Bali with it's lovely, friendly people and beautiful cascading hillsides of rice fields. It also had many small shops with men carving a variety of interesting small wood products, bought some to bring home.

February 2nd, arrived in Singapore, were everything works perfectly. Took some time to organize and send out faxes. By now had accumulated a box of new products which I would order as imports in the future. Sent the box to my son to keep for me until I arrived home. Went to see the medical clients from last year, obtained a small order. There were several companies who wanted me to represent their products in the U.S., so took the information. Visited with Larry and his girlfriend, they were very interested in learning more about the import - export business.

February 18th, arrived in Bangkok, Thailand. Had follow up meetings with medical companies, but no orders. At the hotel, met a gentleman who had a factory in northern Thailand making beautiful small cane and silk boxes. Gave him a large order, because knew they would sell. The items were so unique and beautiful, they sold at museums in Florida.

February 24th, left for Bombay, India. My previous medical contacts did not appear to be interested in purchasing products. Did find lovely handmade products, purchased more imports. February

27th, took the train to Delhi, this was a delightful experience. Stayed in a cabin, a gentleman dressed in very proper English clothing, with white gloves, served me afternoon tea. Checked on a few companies, but there was not much business in Delhi, it was mostly government. The next day traveled to Agra to see the Taj Mahal. This was spectacular monument of love for his wife, it was about a two hour ride outside Delhi. Oh! it was breathtakingly beautiful and a **must see**.

March 4th, taken out to dinner by some people I had met. At the airport, because of some scamming with the exit fee, was upgraded to first class. It would have been great on this long ride, however became very sick with food poisoning. So much for the 1st class free drinks and food, darn!!

March 8th, arrived in Zagreb, Yugoslavia. Took a taxi from the airport. After circling the same area three times told the taxi to stop. Drew a circle around three times. He understood at I knew what he was doing. The hotel was right down the block. They were no longer under Communist control and much was new for them. At the time, it was difficult to negotiate business. Checked for the date of the Rotary meeting, thought perhaps they could give me information on the business climate. The meeting was very different from the usual. It was in the evening and cost US$ 32. They had a menu which started with wine, a full course meal and then discussion. I sat next to an American Express man who was interpreting every thing for me. After dinner was a political discussion on what was happening in Yugoslavia. They felt war was about to break out, which it did within the year.

The AmEx man said the man across from me, Ivan Lackovic, the second most famous artist in Yugoslavia. Asked how could he be the second most famous? He said in respect for his teacher who was still alive. When the meeting was over Ivan gave me his sketches on the menu. He wanted to know what I did, the AmEx man did all the translations. A few days later, received a message from the hotel desk that Ivan would be over to the hotel at 10: a.m. tomorrow morning to bring me some marketing materials. He wanted me to represent him in Florida. Went down to the lobby a few minutes early and noticed every staff member was there. They had made a big semicircle, the manager explained that Ivan was famous in Zagreb. When Ivan arrived, he gave me a hug and cheek kiss - kiss, like we were old friends. He had a bag with some of his art and other marketing materials.

On the way to Dubrovnik, went to Our Lady of Medjugorje shrine - a very special place. 1981 the Blessed Virgin Mary first appeared to six children with a message of peace and love. I sat on a rock up on the hill where Mary appeared. It was a very memorable religious experience.

Then on to the beautiful Dubrovnik, a walled-in village with culture, art, music, many old buildings and beautiful people. The streets looked like polished marble. Saw many pieces of art by Ivan Lackovic. It was there I found his book. A beautiful printed book titled IVAN LACKOVIC, the unique YUGOSLAV NAIVE ART. Tried to get in touch with Ivan after I talked with a museum curator who was interested in his work. I had no luck reaching him at any of the contact numbers he had given me. Ivan seemed like such a nice man. Was sorry to hear, sometime later, he had been killed in the war. His very unique, beautiful painting of a woman holding a huge bouquet of yellow tulips, the one he had given me in the hotel as a sample, is now framed and hangs on my living room wall.

Ivan Lackovic painting

March 23rd, arrive by train in Budapest, Hungary at 11:30 p.m. The train station was dirty and there was no help anywhere. Finally found a taxi to the hotel. The next day, decided to look up my Grandmother Baba's maiden name in the phone book. She was from Hungary, hers was a very common last name. Unfortunately didn't have any luck tracking down my relatives, most did not speak English and I did not speak Hungarian.

Once again, Rotary was the best help for business contacts. They told me, most of the successful business people in all the ex Communist foreign countries spoke English. They gave me a number of medical leads which I contacted and left the marketing materials but they where not used to buying products. Up to then, most products were done as an exchange with Russia or other Communist countries.

Hungary has two areas, on one side of the Danube River is Buda the other Pest, there was a slight difference. On the Buda side I went to large natural springs and tried to talk with the women. They were friendly, wanted to talk but no one spoke English. On the Pest side, there was art everywhere and a number of beautiful old buildings.

While visiting a museum, met a very talented metal artist, Walter Madarassy. Wanted to buy one of his artistic coins but he couldn't come up with a price. He invited me to his home, with many wonderful pieces of his sculpture. Met his very nice family and we shared some tea. After a pleasant couple of hours left with hopes he might sell me some of his artwork. No luck.

Behind my hotel Taverna, was a large open sidewalk where Russians laid out their blankets, to put their black-market goods brought from Russia. When they saw the police coming, they would quickly picked up their blankets and run. I did buy ten men's watches with different Russian pictures on the face of the watch. I kept one as a souvenir, it has CCCP and hammer and sickle on the face, it's a Peterhof windup and it still works. Wish I had bought more, they sold like hot cakes.

April 2nd, Prague, Czechoslovakia met with Gabriela at the Ministry of Health, she was very interested in the medical products. Left three samples and flyers for her to show the doctors. Gabriela and I met for lunch a few times. She wanted to learn more about doing business, Hospice and personal women to women talk. I agreed to her invitation to return and participate in her Hospice seminar, she would arrange housing for me.

Prague had this wonderful town square with great architectural buildings and the Old Town Astronomical Clock Tower. People would gather a little before the hour to watch it's movements. While waiting, turned to the man beside me to ask where he was from, he said he was from Russia. Also asked him, what did he did in Russia, in perfect English, he told me he was in the KGB, secret service. I said "would you still have a job with the breakup of the Communist world?" He responded "don't know." Then the clock started to move which ended the conversation while everyone watched the magnificent clock's movements. When it was finished moving noticed the Russian man was no longer there.

April 6th Warsaw, Poland. Took the overnight train there for an appointment the next day with the commercial attache at the Embassy. Unlike the other countries, the businesses were looking to privatize and form joint ventures. They were ready and anxious to do business. Warsaw was very bleak and cold, with big wide streets and very large Russian statues. One of the contacts the Embassy gave me was a medical company, Kamed. They were very interested in developing a joint venture with an American company. Kamed had given me a stethoscope to bring back, asked a doctor I knew to use it, she was very impressed. My company was not interested in a joint venture.

April 15th, left Warsaw for Frankfurt, Germany. My business trip was over. Spent time visiting and stayed with a number of friends who lived in different areas of Germany. First visited with two ladies I had met through an adult organization called Friendship Forces, who had previously stayed with me in Florida. Carla, a teacher in Dusseldorf, took me to visit her class, the students enjoyed the chance to practice their English. Roswita, lived in Gelsenkirchen, both took me touring all around their area of Germany. Then also visit two opera singers who had rented a place where I lived in Florida. She was the diva in the Essen Opera and he was the male lead in Hannover Opera. Went to an opera in both cities, heard them practice, la, la, la, la, la. It was such fun, arrived home May 2.

There was much followup work to do. My days were full going to the medical companies concerning sales and further training.

January 1992, most everything was organized and had sometime to play tennis again. During that time was introduced to Paul, from Paris, on the tennis court. At the time, he was working in Florida for a Germany company. We became good friends.

Also, had time to do some sailing with a Windjammer group in Clearwater. Continued doing volunteer work at Hospice.

* * * *

Trip Four May 4, 1992

picture of Paul

Upon arriving in Budapest, Hungary, moved on to Prague for the Hospice seminar had promised Gabriela last year. She had arranged for me to move into a typical apartment where the local people lived. It was laid out like a box, the walls inside only went up about six feet for room divides. It had a living room, one bedroom and a bathroom, it was sparse but comfortable. It was an opportunity to see how the locals lived. At the seminar met Karl from Germany. He asked if I would return to Germany with him and speak at his Hospice seminar, I did. While telling the people at the seminar about Hospice, it's palliative care, keeping the patient medicated so they are free of pain in their last days, a woman raised her hand, "Vee in Germany do not like to die," she announced in a firm voice. I noticed Karl was hiding behind some papers laughing. I tried to keep a straight face and told her, "We in the United States do not like to die either." Have never forgotten that experience.

Returned home May 24, was having trouble walking, my knee was very swollen and could not bend it. Went to the doctor the next day, he drained a lot of fluid out of my knee.

It's time for me to do some careful evaluation of my international business. The Export part, was not very successful, with the exception of the one big sale. Trade fairs would have cost less in travel and might have produced more business. However, for me, it was not only about making money, I wanted to learn about different cultures, talk with the people in the countries and learn about their customs. Although their homes, faces and customs were different then mine, they all wanted the same thing; family, food and a place to live in peace. I did go to many more countries than on the original list and met many delightful, helpful, kind people everywhere I went, thank you God. This was invaluable, could not have experienced this any other way. It has been a wonderful experience, very thankful.

The Import business was fun. The products all sold very well but would it be enough to live a comfortable life?

So, what about you? This was one of my dreams, any ideas on what you want to do to change your life. Life does not give us guaranties ... what matters is what we do with it.

"I've never been poor, only broke. Being poor is a frame of mind. Being broke is only a temporary situation." - Mike Todd

Chapter Six

Changes Again

After much thought, it was time to find a nine to five job and earn a regular pay check, darn. Enjoyed my time traveling.

After numerous interviews, finally found a job. Had hoped it would be teaching at Schiller University but it was an office job. Would need a Masters degree to teach at the University level. After work, met with the Dean at Tampa College about credits and courses needed to get a Masters degree in International Business. Already had graduate certification in Evaluation and Special Education from the University of South Florida. With the credits I had it would be possible to complete the Masters by the end of the summer taking two classes each semester in the evenings after work. Signed up and paid the fees. I now worked full time at Schiller, then attended evening classes.

February 16, 1993 was returning home in the rain after class, the last thing I remembered was waiting to make a left turn. Then heard someone knocking on my car window telling me not to move, an ambulance was on the way. The man told me I was hit head-on by a car, spun around and my car totaled. At the time, owned a '85 Mercedes and was told if I were in a smaller car I would have died. Do not have any memory of the accident, must have fallen asleep, I thank *God* to be alive. In the ambulance and at the hospital I was in and out of consciousness. Was taken for X-rays and then finally to a hospital room, where I fall asleep. The next day my son Chip, who lives in Tallahassee was there. He had already been to the police and got the accident report. Then to the car compound and took pictures of the car. Black and blue marks continued to appear all over my body; arms, knees, stomach, etc. Along with a very bad clavicle break, there were three broken ribs on my right side, punctured sternum and right lung, left shoulder and arm problems. Had been admitted to the hospital on a Tuesday night and by Friday they had completed all they could do. The hospital staff asked my son if he would be at home with me, he said yes, so was sent home. Had to stay in a type of harness 24/7 except for a daily shower of ten minutes. Chip and his fiancée, Lynda, set up my bed with all kinds of pillows for some comfort. Both took care of food, but they needed to leave on Sunday to get back to work. Chip knew my neighbor, Joyce. He arranged for her to come down daily for me a take a shower and change of clothes. Thanks to Joyce, those ten minutes in the shower were the best time of the day.

Monday, Schiller University called wondering where I was, told them my problem In order to keep getting paid, they brought some work for me to do at the condo until I could return to the office. That was okay with me, didn't want to lose my pay check.

The following Wednesday, called the college and spoke with the Dean. They arranged to have someone bring over my course material and worked with me on taking tests, etc. They where most helpful until I finally return to campus.

Went every two or three weeks for X-rays on my clavicle, it was not coming together, it was still about one and half inches apart. My priest, Fr. Jim who had been visiting, decided we needed to meditate on the clavicle. We asked the angels to help push the two clavicle bones together.

March 30th, my friend Karl and family decided they would still come as planned, perhaps they could help. Encouraged them to go to Disney with the children for a day or two. When they returned, it was time for another X-ray and Karl wanted to come with me. While I was getting a new X-ray, Karl and the doctor talked. The doctor told him he did not know what they were going to do about my situation because the harness was not do the job. Then they looked at the new X-ray and were confused. There was now something coming out of the two bones towards each other. I told them about Fr. Jim's meditation and they didn't know what to say. For me, it was believing in the wonders of *God and his angels* and the help of my friend, Fr. Jim.

After some time, rented a car, got back to work part time and to school. I did complete the Masters Degree in International Business.

Prior to the accident, had sold my condo to the two opera singers from Germany. Now they were ready to move in, I had to move out. Rented a place in this condo on the fifth floor until August to give me some time to figure out what next. Originally, before the accident, my plans were to go to Sarasota to live, however felt the time was not right. Wanted to get away. Decided to live and work in France. Called my friend, Paul in Paris, asked him if he could find me a small place to live in Strasbourg. This area was close to a number of other European countries and perhaps allow me to take short trips to Germany, Switzerland and Austria. Paul found a place, August 2nd, 1993 departed for Strasbourg. The apartment owners picked me up at the airport, was very grateful. It had been a long trip, was very tired, hurt everywhere and my right knee was stiff. The apartment was very simple but would certainly do for now.

Rested most of the next day except for going out to find a grocery store. Was more tired than in the past from trips, did a lot of resting/sleeping the next few days. Took a city tour to get some bearings of the city. After a week or so, attended a Rotary Club meeting where I met a very nice couple, Judy and Monte who invited me to their home. Between Rotary, the American Conciliate and the International Women's club, met a number of interesting, nice people who took me to a variety of places in town.

It was time to be creative again, found it was too expensive to rent an apartment, buy food and do things with the women. Decided to check out the Holiday Inn, which had an indoor swimming pool and presented my idea. Room and meals, in exchange, teach for three months, 12 hours of job related English for the staff. The Manager was amused with the idea and would give it some thought. Heard from him the next week, they are interested however did not want to start the program until December. Met again with the manager, Oliver, to work out all the details of the program. Everything was explained, all the details worked out, would start December 1st, 1993.

The ladies in Strasbourg were very active, they had activities all the time and always included me. We took trips to art galleries, a boat cruise and invites to dinner.

In the meantime heard from Karl, they were offering a beginner business German class, why not come, stay with his family for a month. Well, was really enjoying all the people and activities in Strasbourg but it was costly. Told everyone I would be back in December. Looked forward to seeing everyone again, going to visit a friend in Germany.

Off to Bremen on the cold North Sea to take a supposed to be, business German class to help with doing business. The class turn out to be a college Freshman German class.

Before I left Florida my son, Chip and his fiancee, Lynda were planning their wedding for the following year. When I called from Karl's, they informed me the wedding was now going to be this September 25th. The reason, Chip was transferred and Lynda found a teaching job where he was transferred. They were holding the wedding at a B & B and fly directly there. It was a fun wedding with karaoke music and lots of dancing.

Now had two months to go somewhere before returning to Strasbourg and the Holiday Inn and needed a place to stay. Decided to return to Indian Rocks Beach, where I knew people. Found a small inexpensive apartment, with a pool, across from the tennis courts. It worked out fine.

Returned to Strasbourg, France November 30. Start classes the next day. These classes were very specific to the jobs the staff did for the Holliday Inn. It had nothing to do with English tenses, etc. If they worked in room service, taught them what to say when they knocked on the door, etc. We pantomimed everything, it was fun. It's amazing how quick they learned when relaxed and having fun. I also got to enjoy the pool and sauna were I stood out like a sore thumb! Was the only person in the sauna with a bathing suit. Oh, us modest Americans!

This program gave me time to enjoy Strasbourg and visit it's many beautiful areas. All the classes where in the afternoons, had mornings to go to meetings and also met people for lunch or dinner.

The manager Oliver, had a staff Christmas party, which I was invited to and given a bonsai tree. Returned to my room with my piece of a special Christmas cake, which had a plastic baby Jesus hidden in it somewhere. The next day went to see the cooks to tell them I got the baby Jesus in my piece of cake. Had blackened my front tooth and with a very serious face, pointed to my blackened tooth. They looked horrified. I waited a minute, then wiped it off, we all had a good laugh.

Christmas in Strasbourg was so festive, real Christmas trees every 50 feet, with gold bows and white lights. There were two Christmas marts with a huge variety of decorations to purchase, which I did. Called my mom and both sons, would miss seeing them for the holidays. Jetta invited me to her home in the country for Christmas day. Another friend picked me up at the hotel. It was so nice of her to invite me, got to experience their typical Christmas dinner. There were four vegetables, salmon and tarts. Afterwards we went for a walk in the snow. I was given a ticket attend a lovely performance of the Budapest Orchestra on the 29th.

New Years Eve went to the Valley of Munster with Yanka. What a night! Crazy games and drinks, such fun. Next day out for a two hour walk in the snow, it was beautiful.

There were so many things to do, shopping trips, concerts, yoga, parties, New Comers Tea, Mystery Night, always something enjoyable to do. The people were very friendly and was always invited to join them at various activities. I mention this so you will realize that going alone to new places does not mean you will be sitting in your hotel room with nothing to do.

Sunday the 16th became very sick. It took a week before I was feeling better. Started to take more saunas. The following Tuesday the ladies took me to the healing waters of Baden Baden, hot warm bubbling waters, it fixed everything. Felt wonderful.

By the end of January classes were going very well, everyone is now speaking some English. The manager, Oliver was very please. He had spoken with the manager in Lyon, Huguette, she wanted me to do the program at her hotel next. The franchise owner of Holiday Inns in France owned a number of hotels and wanted me to do the program at all his hotels. Oh my, what a nice surprise. By the way, you do not need an English degree to do this program, if you are a native English speaker, have stayed at hotels, you can create the program.

Saturday, February 12th a group of us left for Lauterbrunnen, Switzerland and a ski/snow weekend. It was a picturesque town, high up in the mountains. I'm not a skier but it was enjoyable walking around, did buy a SWATCH watch. Took a train ride to Interlaken. For me it was a new, fun experience.

Monday afternoon February 21st, was asked to come down to a meeting room, *surprise!* They had a thank you, going away party for me. There on the table, was a large HERMES bag, on top of the bag one of their magazines showing a variety of scarves. I laughed and said "thanks, like I really can afford one to their scarves." There was a variety of different small gifts from all the different class groups. The one from the kitchen staff was a set of windup, chopper teeth with a front tooth blacked out, guess they hadn't forgotten my prank. We all laughed. There on the bottom of the bag, beautifully wrapped was a HERMES-PARIS scarf from the manager, Oliver. What a beautiful scarf and very generous gift. Was shocked with everything, what a wonderful and fun experience.

Before leaving had many good-bye calls to make thanking everyone. Strasbourg was a great experience, had no idea when I left Florida what I was going to do. Life's wonderful surprises, if you are open to them. Thank you God.

Thursday the 24th took the train to Lyon. A man from the hotel picked me up at the station. Met with Huguette, then to my room where a box of candy was waiting for me. The next day talked with the staff, explained the program and organized the schedule.

My favorite class was the kitchen staff of cooks, perhaps because I liked to eat. They often had me sample their new dinner combos. A young sales person staying at the hotel, came over to talk with me when I finished my dinner one evening. He asked if he could sit with me during dinner while he was staying there. He seemed nice enough so said sure. He would wait to see what I received for dinner before he ordered. If it looked good he would ask the waiter if he could have the same. I asked myself if that was the reason he wanted to sit with me? Not my wonderful personality!

While I was there some of the kitchen staff where going to the Duboeuf Vineyard to taste and purchase the new beaujolais. They asked if I wanted to join them. They were going in the morning and would be back in time for classes so joined them. They received a warm welcome upon arrival, they were known there. The winery owner asked who I was. When it was time to leave was given a Duboeuf apron and a magnum of beaujolais. Again, another pleasant surprise, from generous, nice people.

During this time, my son, Michael was telling me about how people were breaking into his store at night and robbing it. After speaking with the police, he was considering getting a gun and staying in the store. Really don't know what I thought I could do to help but felt I needed to be there. At the same time in Lyon, police in riot gear had set off a gas bomb in front of the Holiday Inn door to break up the demonstrations. Gas came in the hotel. The combination of riots in Lyon and concern for my son, decided to fly to Raleigh, North Carolina on Saturday, April 2nd, 1994. Apologies to Holiday Inn, that I did not complete my agreement. Decided the welfare of my son was more important.

I realized by now that life was a series of unexpected, uncontrollable changes ...so ... roll with them. What about you, are you ready to roll! God will be there to help, if you ask Him.

"Faith is to believe what you do not see; the reward of faith is to see what you believe."
                                                                                    - Saint Augustine

Chapter Seven

North Carolina and other places

April 2, 1994 arrived in Raleigh. My son, Michael had already setup a place in the back of his showrooms to live. We put my bags into his apartment located just up the road, then went down to see his business. He had an upscale custom made leather goods store. There were a few things where I might be able to help. Seeing as he had help in the store, he decided to show me a little of Raleigh. It had many art galleries for the artists in the community. Michael knew, art was a passion of mine. Raleigh looked like a really nice city. We spent some time back at the store and then walked back to his/my "new" apartment to organize. Michael seemed pleased to see me, I know I was glad to see him.

Once again, had much to reorganize now that I was back in the states. Divided my time at the store and apartment. On the 15th, Michael and I drove up to Greensboro, NC to visit my mom, she was so glad to see us. We returned to Raleigh the next day and I went down to Indian Rocks, Florida where I arranged to have my belongings sent to me. Back in Raleigh again, went down to the store. Started meeting a variety of nice people, there was plenty to do. Once Michael moved into the back of the store, he let it be know he had a gun. The break-ins stopped. After some time, we realized there was not much for me to do at the store. On May 30th, bought a used Chevy Blazer, it sat-up high, felt safe. While still helping out some at the store, began looking for a full time job. Also did some fun things with new friends, by taking a weekend trip to the beach, attended many events at art galleries. We also took a pre Christmas trip to the Biltmore Estate in Asheville. This is a must see, it's unbelievably beautiful at Christmas.

On September 14th, about 10:30 a.m. I was going down a one way street in Raleigh. A woman who was very busy talking with her friend turned down the street, going the wrong way and crashed right into me. There was damage to both cars. For me, back and neck pain. The woman admitted she was at fault and took care of all the expenses. The trauma of another car accident, driving once again became very difficult for me.

On September 6th, had an interview at the World Trade Center in Durham, about a half hour from Raleigh. September 26th, was offered the position of Membership Services Director, accepted, started the job October 3. Upon meeting the staff, found out I was the only person who had any actual international business experience. Started a number of new programs to increase membership. The highlight for me, was being sent to the then World Trade Center in New York for a new members information / orientation. Remember looking out the window and seeing small planes flying below between the buildings. It's such a sad memory now.

The lease on Michael's apartment, that I'm living in, would end on December 31. Decided to look for a small apartment in Durham and found an okay place. This will put me ten minutes from my job, less than an hour to Michael' and an hour from my mom in Greensboro. It was in a good location, decided to take the apartment. On December 22, Michael and I go to Greensboro, my mom was in the hospital. We stay over a day, returned to Raleigh to have Christmas dinner with Michael. He then took me to the airport on the 24th and celebrated Christmas with my other son, Chip and wife, Lynda in Tallahassee, Florida.

With many new programs at the WTC, monthly meetings, country seminars, Go Global seminar, education and socials, it was now a very active place. The membership grew, everyone had something to do.

During this time, also started taking various art classes evenings or weekends, started playing tennis again, and took more trips with the ladies.

A year later in October of 1995, decided to take my vacation time. Things were not going so great, the salary offer was not to my liking and there were other issues. It was time to finally look at moving to Sarasota, Florida.

The timing was right, my family are all in healthy positions. Had put Sarasota on hold back in 1986, for my mom when I returned from Peace Corps. Spent time with a real estate agent who found the perfect condo in Sarasota. On the intercostal waterway with a nice pool. Made an offer, it was excepted and the process was in motion.

Returned to work Monday the 16th of October, was called into the bosses office and given the morning to clear out my office, I was fired. Well, didn't have to resign like I had intended to. My friend and confidant Laura, told me, I could collect unemployment, a first for me. It all worked out better than I could have imagined. Had till the end of December to get everything closed up in the Raleigh area. Had garage sales, packed, bought new furniture at the whole sale area of North Carolina. They would ship it to Florida in January. Visited friends to say my goodbyes, spent Thanksgiving with my mom and Michael, Christmas with Michael.

The closing on my condo in Sarasota was December 11th, didn't have to be there. When I was there hired a handy man to take down all the heavy drapes, strip the old wallpaper, remove the carpets, everything was to go. The next step was to clean and paint it. When he finished, he called the carpet company and let them in. Arrived on the afternoon of 28th December, they were just finishing up the carpet. Spent New Years Eve with my realtor. A new start to a New Year 1996.

* * * *

Finally in SARASOTA, Florida, started my long number of job interviews and part time work at a variety of places, too numerous to mention. Would this be all that I had imagined it would be? Was doing seminars on how to start a business and how to go global for Manatee Community college.

Started dating some very nice men, but no one special. One belonged to a Yacht club, it was fun to do some sailing again. Also back playing tennis a couple times a week. Volunteered at a number of Art organizations and helped out with a weekend golf tournament for Cancer. All said and done, it was a very busy time in my life.

Had taken a variety of Art classes in North Carolina and enjoyed them. It's was now 1997, perhaps it was time to try to pursue art as a business, another dream of mine. A weekend class in Shibori, the ancient technique of dying fabric sounded interesting. The fabric could be folded, twisted, clamped, crushed or hand-sewn and then given numerous dye baths of different colors. It was a lot of work but the results were so varied and original. In the class made connections with other fabric artists for the new art project.

Look Good - - Feel Good, this is how you will see yourself when you purchase from TAM's group of American Wearable Fiber Artists. All articles were sold exclusively at fashion shows, benefits, home parties and private functions. There were four artists and myself, each had a specialty product. Margaret made *Clings,* original hand-painted silk chiffon georgette vests and scarves, in many shapes and fantasies. Kim, produced the most elegant, beautifully hand-painted silk Kimonos. Jane made fabulous *shibori scarves,* hand-sewn for shape and color control. Deb, produced hand bags using pieces of silk from Jane. Resa, which was my artist name, hand-dyed silk scarfs unique in design and color very different than Jane's.

I designed a color postcard with product pictures on the front, all the details on the back and sent them to numerous organizations and groups in Sarasota. The response was fantastic! The project was off the ground. The artists were producing new articles and everyone enjoyed receiving pay checks.

Having been in the Peace Corps, knew the Embassy people would be interested in seeing, "hand-made in America" products. Faxed the Embassy in Paris, France and London, England both said yes. Left for France April 14th, 1997, stayed with my friend, Paul. On the 16th had a sale at the Embassy, they were so pleased to have the opportunity to buy beautiful silk articles of clothing made by American artists. Sales were fantastic. On the 18th went with Paul, down to a small town in southern France to visit with some of his friends. We enjoyed walking down to the market on Saturday for delicious fresh food. After a fun time returned to Paris Sunday and visited my other friend, Mondher that evening. Some people at the Embassy had called, they wanted to see me again on Tuesday to purchase a few more articles. Went to the Embassy, then took the Eurostar, fast train, through the Chunnel to London. A tennis friend, Barry and his wife, Margaret invited me to stay at their home in the country. Took the train into London for the sale at the London Embassy on the 25th. The staff there were also pleased to purchase hand-made products made in America, once again sales were excellent. By the way, there is good food made by the English. Barry and Margaret took me to some wonderful pubs where we enjoyed some delicious English fare, yum. On the 28th, we went to the Tower of London, viewed the Crown Jewels. Jewels, jewels, jewels, each more beautiful than the other. Then on to the Coventry Market and out to dinner. Left London, arrived in Sarasota on April 30th. It was a very successful trip, wrote out checks to all the artists.

silk sale in London

Kept busy making my scarves and also taking a few other art classes. Sumie art was one of my favorites, was going to try using the process on my silk scarves. We usually had a show about once a month, which kept us all busy making new wearable art. Then Kim, the artist who made the kimonos, told me she no longer wanted make the kimonos or work with silk. Could not find a replacement and so ended this project, I was really disappointed. The curve balls of life.

Was now teaching two night classes, Retailing and Advertising at Manatee Community College, along with a variety of seminars for them.

On May 17th, 1998 my Mom had a fall and died after being brought to the hospital. It was sudden and a very difficult time for an already divided family, as mentioned when my Dad died.

1999 continued doing much of the same work and included some volunteer work at the hospital and Angel flight. This is a group of pilots who fly small planes taking burn victims to the specialized hospitals. I rode along to assist.

Received some unexpected money from my fathers Will, which had never been settled and decided to join the Bird Key Yacht Club. This club had clay tennis courts, boating and was five minutes from my home. There where many enjoyable activities.

One morning in 2000, while reading the paper, saw an advertisement for an Elderhostel trip to China. Always wanted to see China, this time would go with a group, not like 1989, by myself. Signed up for the trip. This was a well organized excursion into China. We all met at the Beijing Airport on September 1st, 2000. We spent three nights in Beijing. Went to Tiananmen Square (now sectioned off to prevent large gatherings), Great Wall, Ming Tombs, Forbidden City and ate lunch at a Szechuan restaurant. We continued on to Temple of Heaven, a Friendship store (which had very little in it) and for dinner, the delicious, finger licking good, Peking Duck. The next day we toured the Summer Palace and Beijing zoo, to see its pandas. All the buildings were unbelievable, especially when you think about the time period they were built.

September 4th, we flew to Qingdao for ten days of cultural education. We were taught Qi Gong, Tai Chi, Chinese Calligraphy, lectures and Chinese painting. We were given tours of this beautiful seaside city, the Pier and Xiao Qing Dao island, took a swim in the clean, clear, cool Yellow Sea. Went to the Tsingtao Brewery, to sample some good German beer, built when the large German community lived there. Then to the Tsingtao department store and the Jimolu Free market for some great buys. Field trip to Shiren fishing village, Children's Palace and Tsingtao Museum. Was very impressed with the large metal sculptures everywhere. One day while getting a foot massage, by a gentleman who spoke English, he asked me what I did in the States. Told him I taught at a college, he asked me if I would teach at a college in Qingdao. Asked for his card and said would think about it.

September 14th, three nights in Xian. The first day we visited the Hui (Moslem) district, street markets with many different, inexpensive, gift things, Great Mosque and Drum Tower and exquisite Dumpling Dinner. Next day Banpo Museum and Terra Cotta Warriors. Each warriors face was different, what an unbelievable project! In the evening, a performance of Tang dynasty Music and Dance.

September 17th Shanghai for two days. We visited the YuYuan Gardens, Garden of Leisurely Happiness and the old original sections of Shanghai. In the evening Shanghai Acrobatics Performance, with their amazing grace and skill. The following day we visited the Shanghai Fine Arts Museum and lunched at Long Hua Temple, then walked on the Bund. Across the river was Pudong, with all the new contemporary architecture, that you now see when newscasts talk about Shanghai.

We departed the next day for home, it was a fantastic trip, learned so much. This country has such diversity and the people are curious, they want to talk with you.

A few days after my return, went down to Manatee Community College to speak with Jim, Business Department head, about the offer to teach in China. He thought it would be a very interesting experience. So, why not! Faxed my resume to the massage man. Three days later received a call from Qingdao Institute of Architecture and Engineering, telling me a teacher had quit and wanted to know, when could I come.

There were many forms to fill out including special teaching Visa applications from China. My neighbor next door, wanted to know if his mother could rent my condo while I was gone. It wasn't something had intended to do but thought why not? So I did. Everything ready, leave for Qingdao November 10th, 2000.

As you might have noticed by now, I was a restless person, who wanted to learn about the world and it's people by experiencing it. Being open to possibilities, who is to know God's ways. His ways, for me, have been very interesting opportunities. Always thankful, now started a new dream adventure.

Are you still thinking about making changes but have not done anything? What are you waiting for? Nothing has convinced you yet that *you* can change your life. If you are still in your unhappy place, maybe you want to be there? Perhaps you prefer to be a victim so people will feel sorry for you. YOU have to decide to take a chance, nothing happens if you do nothing.

"You can't always get what you want, but if you try sometimes, you might find, you get what you need." The Rolling Stones

"If at first you don't succeed, try, try again." - William E. Hickson

Chapter Eight

Living and Working in China

November 12, 2000 arrived in Qingdao, China, at noon on Sunday. Was picked up at the airport by Lou, my wyban, the person in charge of my welfare while at the University. There were no apartments available on campus. My apartment was across the street from the campus and had to climb up seven floors. After checking the apartment, saw it had not been cleaned and there was no hot water. Lou decided I should stay at a hotel so they could clean the place and put in some hot water. Definitely agreed with that idea, got to the hotel, took a nice hot shower and fell asleep. Lou called around six pm to take me to dinner. Next morning at nine he arrived at the hotel to take me to meet the English department staff to discuss my classes. At eleven went to my apartment to organize and clean, clean, clean. The weather had turned cold so they brought me a small heater. Two days later finally had hot water. It sure was nice to have a warm shower.

picture of bathroom

Started meeting my classes which included thirty plus students. All had picked English names, thank goodness. Also met the other English teacher, Mary, a nun from Ireland who had a nice ground floor apartment, on campus.

The young adults in the classes were great students. The University also asked me to do a class for any students interested in learning how to start a business and / or international business. Over 70 students signed up for the class. Teaching here was easier than in Florida, here the students wanted to learn, they were so quiet you could hear a pin drop. I had brought many teaching materials with me, a book with pictures was a great help. After a very short time, I realized the importance of taking everything with me when I left in the morning. The seven flight of stairs were enough once a day.

Pictures on campus:

students in one of my classes

small store with a little bit of everything

small store with fresh vegetables

*grandpa with his grandchild
and small fold-up seat*

mom toilet training child

The child's pants had a hole, every hour the mother had the child squat to go to the bathroom. By the age of one, they told me the child was toilet trained. P.S. this was before disposable diapers.

Mary took me to a small shopping area within walking distance. We were a novelty, the only caucasians in the area. Mothers would point at us so their children would look. Below are pictures of the area where we lived. On the way to the store or park you would see the following scenes.

men out on the street giving hair cuts

fixing your shoes as you wait

43

cooking on the street, delicious sweet potatoes in the big use oil barrels

the men would bring their birds out in cages to hang on the line, while they would sit on little fold up chairs and play cards or other games.

Then down to the park where you would see an area with a record player, women all dressed up and in heels, men with ties ballroom dancing.

another area men sitting playing instruments

another area doing Beijing Opera

Had wanted to take a field trip with the business class to see the Nike factory. I was doing some English teaching for Nike so it was okay with them. However the English department said no, that I must be a spy. It didn't make any sense to me, they ended up sending us to a Chinese factory instead, to spy, I guess! The students were very disappointed, everything was old.

students at the factory

Right behind my apartment was a Senior Center that had art classes. Asked a Chinese teacher to come with me so she could ask if I could take a class. At first they said no, I didn't speak the language. Explained that I could watch the teacher and then try to copy. After much discussion, I was allowed and ended up taking two classes. The local paper heard about it, came and took pictures. This was a first for them.

one of my classes

picture in the paper

teacher giving me a good bye picture

Went down to the Holiday Inn in the newer section of Qingdao to present the barter arrangement for Spring break. This would give me a place to live plus meals. After much on and off with the General Manager Peter, the project was a go, start teaching twelve hours a week, January 15th. Attended the ExPat community luncheon on the 17th. It was a large community, most were living in modern apartment facilities with pool, tennis courts, etc. very nice.

new modern area of Qingdao

staff party

Chinese New Year was the 24th, fireworks everywhere. The Holiday Inn had their Annual Staff Party, it was a lot of fun, music, dancing, silly games.

Returned to campus February 18th when classes resumed. There were some difficult times when I felt lonely but knew my son, Michael was coming. April 5th, just before he came, Lou found a small fourth floor apartment on campus. It was small but much more convenient.

The evening of April 16th met Michael at the Beijing airport as he arrived from Raleigh, North Carolina. He had researched the areas he wanted to see, we tried to utilize public transportation when possible. We climbed some small hills behind the Forbidden City where you could see the vast size of this magnificent palace, then went inside. We came out into Tiananmen Square.

Michael did not want to see the Great Wall at Badaling, it had been rebuilt, had many venders and all the tourists went there. Instead, we hired a taxi to go to a portion of the wall that was still original. Michael crossed the top of a small dam and then scramble up the side of the hill. He climbed up the broken section of the wall, then hiked along the Great Wall by himself, it was too difficult for me.

white dot is Michael walking along wall

Michael climbing up wall

Michael returned with me to the campus on the 19th. We were just in time to go with Lou and a bus load to the Kite Festival. What great kites, the one in the picture below even puffed smoke. Michael was always being asked to have their picture taken with him. At the time, it was a rarity to see a man six feet two inches tall.

Michael at the International Kite Festival

kite

Back on campus, took Michael to my classes, the students were anxious to talk with him. Another day we walked down to the shopping area and park. You've seen the pictures, he was amused, fascinated and impressed with what he saw.

Michael, who was the same age as Lou, thought it would be nice if we took him to lunch before he left. Lou picked the place to meet. When we arrived, we were taken to a private room. There were seven other friends of his sitting around a large round table. I was a little confused about that. They ordered the food and then started "gamba" This is where you toast and then have to drink down all that you have in the glass. Well, this went on all during lunch, I did not participate. Next thing, one of Lou's friends got up, walked over to a couch in the room and fell asleep. Upon finishing lunch, I asked for the check but was told no, the guy that fell asleep on the couch had to pay it, Michael held his own. Yet, another interesting experience. The time passed too quickly, Michael left April 24th, to return to Raleigh.

May 20th was invited to a Chinese wedding of people connected to the private school where Terry, an Australian taught. The ceremony started outside, the bride and groom each held a dove, released it and then 100 more were released. Terry and I were included in many of the pictures, was told it was a honor to have an Australian and American at their wedding. Once inside the bride and groom stood in front of their parents and were asked questions. They then made promises. You will notice the bride had a very beautiful western style white dress, yet the parents and many of the guests where dressed very casual.

bride and groom talking with parent

Later she changed to a red dress, which was the traditional color of the wedding dress. They went from table to table for a wedding toast with everyone. When they left the wedding, the bride was now in a beautiful long purple dress,

May 25th at seven a.m. Lou took us by train in the wooden seat section. This was a six hour torture ride, another experience, this one I would have been happy to do without. We then stayed overnight at a small town in a dirty hotel. Next morning, an hour bus ride to Confucius home. Great architecture and a small parade in the court yard of where they say Confucius was buried. We had some free time to shop, found a great small bowl, Lou thought it was from the Ming dynasty. The next day back to school on the torture train.

Confucius burial site

Was very busy all the time, with a number of private students, the senior citizens art classes, activities with the Expats, looking at art outside and in galleries, many fun, interesting experiences. My contract completed, returned to Sarasota July 18th. Yes, think I might like to teach again in China.

* * * *

Chip, Lynda and grandson Alex came down to visit, it was so good to see them. Now to get my life back in order. Was asked to give a number of talks about living and teaching in China, which I did. Made many calls to friends, paid taxes, lunches, bridge, some boating and tennis. Was so anxious to move to Sarasota back in 1986, back then could have looked for a full time teaching job in special education. However, would have missed all the wonderful experiences in China and the other countries. Now it was to late and I really did not have enough money to retire there. Listed my condo with a real estate agent and began looking to teach at a University in Shanghai, China. Fond of teaching in China, lets see what happens. In the mean time, enjoyed my time in Sarasota. Lynda and Alex, my grandchild, now almost two years old, came to visit for a week on two occasions. We enjoy playing on the beach, building sand castles, chasing the birds and wading in the water. Was offered a teaching position at Shanghai Maritime University in Pudong, the new area of Shanghai. My condo did not sell, rented it again to my neighbors mother.

* * * *

August 29th, 2002 left early in the morning for Shanghai, China. Arrived the next afternoon, was picked up at the airport and taken to a nice apartment in a courtyard with four apartments for foreign teachers. Very different from Qingdao in many ways, no wyban, there was no one to look after you. The campus was larger and they had a dinning hall with many different food concessions. Two students, Diana and her boyfriend, Black, came over the next day and took me shopping, which was a big help. At 6:20 p.m. Luan Wei, head of the English department, stopped in to set an appointment for the next day at 1:30 to discuss my teaching schedule. Then the required medicals. Met the three other teachers in the courtyard, two Canadian couples and a British man. The arrangement was very nice and they were friendly. Classes started September 9th, the students were more vocal, affluent and self assured than in Qingdao.

Pudong was a new area of Shanghai, you see this side of the river when there is news on TV. It has all the beautiful, tall buildings, all the building was happening in this area. One day looked out of a class room window, to see six building cranes. The other side on the Huangpu River was the Bund. On the Bund usually saw people walking, selling wares, pulling carts, riding bicycles, or exercising. All the original development was on that side of the river, with many different Embassies and communities.

On the 17th of September the university sent a box of Moon cakes which are traditionally given for the Mid-Autumn Festival. Typical moon cakes are round pastries, with a rich thick filling usually made from red bean or lotus seed paste is surrounded by a thin crust and may contain yolks from salted duck eggs. Moon cakes are usually eaten in small wedges accompanied by Chinese tea. On the 18th our group was taken to dinner. On the 20th three students, representing my classes came over with flowers, a framed picture, another box of Moon cakes and wine. What lovely surprises.

October 1st was China National Day, the university was closed till the 10th. At a bazaar, sold a number of my silk scarves. I had private students, part time work at Holiday Inn and evaluated some students for learning disabilities at a private school. In the courtyard we were always celebrating someones birthday. Went on short trips to different areas to see the river people, textile mill, Silk Museum and up into the tall buildings. The picture is looking down at the Huangpu river.

Huangpu river

One of the people I met worked for Siemens, she invited me on the test run of the bullet train to the airport. Normally a 45 minute drive but on the bullet train it would be only 7 minutes. Off we went, unbelievable, we were going so fast you never felt the sharp embankments, 7 minutes we were at the airport. We waited a few minutes then returned to the station. We arrived back at the station *but* it did not go all the way in and we could not get off. Everything was computerized, my friend was not on the train but working on the computers. About 15 minutes passed, turned to the person beside me and said "bet we have to go back to the airport." He laughed and said "no." Next thing we started to move, back to the airport. The second time back to the station was perfect, great experience.

the bullet train

In April SARS was diagnosed in China and the campus went on lockdown. No one was allowed into the campus, they didn't want the students going out. The teachers were allowed off campus with a mask. It was a very uncertain time with some activities cancelled.

entrance to campus

June 26th, the term was completed, upon leaving China our temperature was taken, no temperature, you could leave. The same procedure happened when arrived home. The people at my condo were worried I could carry the SARS virus and asked me not to use the inside public areas for two weeks. Chip, Lynda and Alex stayed at a hotel. Visited with them at the pool and we ate outside. It was thought to be safe outside.

About a month after arriving back home my condo sold and on July 28th moved my things to storage. It gave me time to say goodbyes,etc. After visiting both Michael and Chip returned back to China.

August 22nd arrived back in Shanghai, for school year 2003 -04. This time I was at a private Christian school, Kindergarten through 6th grade. I had worked with a few of their students last year and was very impressed with the school. At the time they had students from 53 countries each speaking their own language and they were being taught English and Chinese. They were like little sponges, learning both languages. I liked the Principle and the pay was good so accepted the the position as the learning disabilities specialist,. However, he retired and his replacement was a young man with few skills for the job. They also changed my job description. Would now need to take a bus to another school two days a week, increasing my hours by ten more a week. I was sick often with colds, fever, stomach flu, etc. but had to go to work most of the time. Working with the students was enjoyable however soon realized there was a lot of politics at this school. They held a number of parties, such as, Fiesta Party, Christmas bazaars, Christmas concert, Christmas Party. Flew back home to visit Michael and Chip for the holidays, then returned to China and school on January 4th.

January 21st was the start of Spring break, another teacher and myself had decided to go to the world renowned, Bumgarner Hospital in Bangkok, Thailand for complete physicals. Our insurance would cover it. It took two days and was the most complete, well organized physical I have ever had. There were people from many different countries.

On the 24th we went on to visit Ho Chi Minh City in Vietnam. After taking half day tour of Cu Chi tunnel with all it's traps and them bragging about the torture, I did not want to go to the Historical Museum. Instead spent the after noon shopping, bought some beautiful silk, some small original art and on to dinner. Then a full day tour up the Mekong delta in a fast boat. The area was beautiful and the people nice.

Mekong delt

The 28th on to Cambodia where we stayed at the very beautiful Sofitel Royal Angkor Resort. Purchased a three-day pass for the Angkor Temples, one of the wonders of the modern world. Henri Mahout, a French botanist, believing the peasant tales of the fabled city, stumbled across Angkor Wat in 1860. He was stunned by its vast size, soaring towers, dramatic carvings telling the stories of Hindu mythology and endless courtyards, avenues and buildings. Today Angkor stands fully restored and once again occupied by Buddhist monks.

Me and the tree

Angkor Temples and the Monks

February 2nd back to work. Everything was moving along okay and then my left knee started to swell. The swelling made it almost impossible to walk or climb stairs, I needed surgery. Checked out doctors who did this surgery and found a doctor in Singapore. Over the phone discussed the surgery with Dr. Paul Chang, was very impressed. My health insurance would cover the cost. On March 15th arrived at the hospital for pre-op procedures. The operation was at 2:30 the 16th, it turned out to be much longer than expected. My knee was wrapped, swollen and hurt. The physical therapist had me get up and walk with support. The next day they took the bandage off, it was still bleeding and so on. Much to my delight and surprise, received flowers, cake and fruit from a number of friends. My friend in Paris, Paul called a friend of his in Singapore, Peter, who happened to call when the doctor was there. He asked if he could bring over wine, the doctor said it was okay. The knee and pain got better much quicker! Stayed in the hospital two weeks, both the PT and doctor decided I needed to get out of the hospital. The doctor and his wife took me to dinner and the PT took me to Raffles and a Singapore Sling. Boy! what great medical treatment.

Arrived back at my apartment in Shanghai March 29th, the doctor did not want me to return to work until April 12th. Then it was to be part time, Monday, Wednesday and Friday for two weeks and physical therapy the other days. Also went to the Holiday Inn to swim. After some time was back teaching full time, resumed teaching at the Holiday Inn and swam in their pool. Last day of school with students was July 1st, had decided not to return to the school. Instead did returned to the Holiday Inn in September until December to work with the staff and continue with private students.

Before returning to Florida for the summer had asked my son, Chip to arrange a family reunion at the beach for a week. It was nice to have the family together.

Before going back to China I checked with a travel agent, it would cost me $500.00 extra to get a round-the-world ticket, over the cost of a round trip ticket to Shanghai. Decided to do this allowing me one year to travel. I had to go in one direction and list the places I wanted to go but did not have to give the dates. This would give me the opportunity to see old friends and visit a few new places.

* * * *

On August 15, 2004 left for Veracruz, Mexico, stayed at the Intercontinental. It was very beautiful, located on the water, my employee rate$25. a day, this was a nice perk. Had never been there and there really was not much to see so moved on to Mazatlan, Mexico. Stayed at the Holiday Inn Sun Spree resort on the Pacific. Decided to go out with realtors and let them show me around so I could see what the city had to offer. It had an interesting old city with a beautiful International Theatre, a malecon which is a few miles along the water (like a board walk) and a new more modern area, called the Golden Zone. They even had an English paper once a week. The current issue had pictures and an article about pair of condos being built on the malecon. The next day went to see it. The first building A was semi constructed up to the fifth floor. Looked at the show rooms on the first floor, everything was 1st class, with granite kitchen counters, marble in the bathrooms, tile or marble on the floors, great patio that looked over the malecon and the Pacific. Walked up to the fifth floor, which was as high as I wanted to go. Well! they were giving pre-construction SALE prices on building B to be ready to occupy by September of 2006. Had never thought of Mexico as a place to live. I began to check the cost of things in Mazatlan such as grocery stores, fruits and vegetables, restaurants, theatre tickets, all were less expensive. Round trip flights to my sons home about $400. and SALE prices on the condo, maybe I needed to think about this. Got all the information and also had them send it to my sons. They both thought I was crazy.

September 1st, back in Shanghai, China picked up at the airport by Holiday Inn and started teaching English lessons. Also compiled and had printed a number of books for the learning disabled which sold quickly. Holiday Inn had a big October Fest, a lot of fun, the time went by so quick.

November 30th left for Dubai, United Arab Emeritus (UAE) the friend I was going to stay with had a last minute change so we couldn't get together. While I debated what to do, stayed in the airport about ten hours looking around, it's a very modern place, hotel prices very costly. On to Turkey, took an afternoon cruise on the Bosporus river which was interesting, many of the homes had boat garages.

Turkey boat garage

The views were great from the boat. Next day booked a full day tour, which started good, then we went to a carpet store and the tour continued on without me, disaster. I knew a woman alone in Turkey was not safe. The taxi driver did not take me to my hotel, he stole my money and I had to walk to the hotel. I was so upset did not get the taxi number or his name, so could not do anything. Wanted to get out of Turkey, called my friend Paul in Paris to see if I could come sooner, He told me to make a reservation, let him know when I would arrive and he would be at the airport. The soonest I could leave was December 4th, so took a safe sightseeing tour the next day.

Had a wonderful time in Paris, left for home the 13th of December.

Really thank God for my time in China, for me it was such a learning experience. Saw places never knew about, met interesting people, learned various customs and once again, was pleasantly surprised how friendly and nice people are in a variety of countries.

"A man who wants to do something will find a way, a man who doesn't will find an excuse" Stephen Dooley, Jr.

"Try and fail, but don't fail to try." - Stephen Kaggwa

Chapter Nine

Mexico

Arrived from Paris to my son, Chip, in Tallahassee, FL for Christmas. Then to Michael in St. Louis where I stayed for two months and had medical work.

When I was in China decided to purchase the condo at Las Gavias in Mazatlan, Mexico.

March 1st, 2005 arrived in Guadalajara, Mexico to start a temporary job teaching English and take Spanish lessons. There were many things to see and do, went to Tonala and Tlaquepaque to buy Mexican products for my condo. The older students with cars took me to a number of fun places. On Fridays a friend and I went to eat, drink and listened to the Mariachi band.

Mariachi band

Worked there until summer, then went to Mazatlan to check on my new condo and buy the necessary appliances, new condos only had a stove. Returned to Sarasota, Florida to arrange for my furniture in storage to be moved to Mexico. Spent some time with both sons and then back to Mazatlan, where I took a temporary rental in the old city. This gave me the opportunity to meet many of the people who lived in Mazatlan, most went down to the square to eat at the many delicious restaurants. Joined the Day of the Dead parade and followed the beer wagon through the old city to look at the alters for deceased relatives, interesting and fun.

Day of the Dead Alter

Day of the Dead Parade

Mazatlan also has a large fishing fleet and Tuna canning factory. Mazatlan canned tuna is the best tasting tuna I have ever had.

fishing fleet

October 14th, 2006 moved into las Gavias, building B and my condo. All the appliances and bed that I had purchased were already in the condo so could start living in my beautiful new home. Sitting on the patio with a glass of wine at sunset, you just could not beat it. I looked down on a huge pool with beach chairs, the Malecon with skaters, walkers, joggers, etc. Then miles of beautiful, white sandy beach, often there were dolphins or fish jumping, surfers, para sailing and fireworks on holidays.

son Chip and grandson Alex surfing during their visit

view from patio

Mazatlan has a big Carnival, miles of fantastic floats and parties everywhere, the Mexicans do know how to party!!

Carnival

My seven years in Mexico where most enjoyable. For the most part the people were helpful and friendly. Sometimes, if they do not know the answer to something, they will make up an answer. They say Mexico is a Catholic country, however, in Mazatlan, the week before Easter Sunday which is Holy week, they had their holiday. The beaches are covered with tents and families right up to the sea. Everyone asks me about the cartel, yes, I did see people who had been killed by them. But they will not bother you, I always felt safe in Mazatlan.

There were many activities, water aerobics, wine groups, community movie/theatre, and Charity functions. Bus trips were available to different cities to shop and visit. It seemed we were always busy with something. The theatre had great international programs and the Symphony in Cullican put on a program in Mazatlan monthly. You could find a large variety of food to satisfy your palate at a variety of prices. All in all had a wonderful experience, always open to opportunities, I thank God for presenting it.

sunset from my patio

So, you might be asking why I decided to move? Well, a few things had changed, I was missing my family and the cost to return had more than doubled. Other costs were increasing and medical problems were developing. It was time to return to the states.

Are you trying new experiences? Are you enjoying your life? What are you concerned about? Wish I could meet you and we could talk about it.

"Failure doesn't mean you are a failure... it just means you haven't succeeded yet." - Robert Schuller

"In the end, the only people who fail are those who don't try." - David Viscott

Chapter Ten

In Closing

God has given us life ... it's important what we do with it. My life, for me has been fantastic. I learned about a variety of different cultures with unusual, interesting ways. It seemed there was never a dull moment and was always surprised by how nice people were everywhere I traveled. I am very thankful to my Creator. When I was stuck in a situation, sitting quiet, breathing slow and talking with God an answer would come.

Not all would enjoy my kind of life however *if you want to change your life YOU can. It is up to you, YOU have to make the changes.* If I could do it, you can. We all have choices in life and I do know it is not easy to make changes. Nothing is certain, nothing is guaranteed. So maybe you fail at first BUT at least you tried. Hopefully you learned from it and the next time will be a success. Don't worry about your friends, if they are real friends they will congratulate you for trying.

Try meditating or talking with your God and be open to possibilities. Think about what it is you want and then work hard to get it. There is always a way. Throughout this book I have shared suggestions and different ways that I accomplished my desires. Many can be easily adapted to something you want to do in life. If you want to ...You can.

I hope everyone who reads this book is enjoying their life to the fullest or will be. Now, I am living in central Florida. When I would tell people something about my life, they would say "you need to write a book" and so, here is my book, We Can because **We Think** We Can. My hopes are for you now, may you fully enjoy your life also. Make it count for you and perhaps others. I lived the life I dreamed, now I hope this book will help you live the life YOU want.

"You always pass failure on your way to success." - Mickey Rooney

"There are two types of people who will tell you that you cannot make a difference in this world: Those who are afraid to try themselves, and those who are afraid that you will succeed."
- Ray Goforth

"Let everyone try and find that as a result of daily prayer he adds something new to his life, something with which nothing can be compared." - Mahatma Gandhi

Printed in the United States
by Baker & Taylor Publisher Services